COME AND WORSHIP

Independent Catholic Missal

ACCORDING TO THE USE OF
THE AUTOCEPHALOUS CATHOLIC CHURCH OF ANTIOCH

Copyright © 2013 Leon Roger Hunt

Autocephalous Catholic Church of Antioch

All rights reserved.

ISBN-10: 1492238503
ISBN-13: 978-1492238508

Cover Icon
HOLY THEOTOKOS ENTHRONED
Courtesy of Studio of 'Theophanis the Cretan'
www.eikonografos.com
Used with Permission

PREFACE - page 1

THE LITURGICAL YEAR - page 3

THE MASS

ASPERGES - page 11
VIDI AQUAM - page 13
ORDER OF MASS 1 - page 15
ORDER OF MASS 2 - page 45
ORDER OF MASS 3 - page 68
INTROIT TEXTS - page 91
GOSPEL ACCLAMATIONS - page 104
PREFACES - page 108
OFFERTORY TEXTS - page 121

OFFICES

OFFICE OF PRIME - page 127
OFFICE OF VESPERS - page 136
OFFICE OF COMPLINE - page 143

RITE OF BAPTISM - page 155
VISITATION OF THE SICK - page 166
CONFESSION - page 181
FUNERAL RITE - page 183

COLLECTS & READINGS

TEMPORAL CYCLE - pages 197-270

Advent - page 197
Nativity - page 199
Epiphany - page 201
Time before Lent - page 203
Lent - page 204
Maundy Thursday - page 212
Good Friday - page 221
Holy Saturday - page 227
Easter - page 249
Pentecost - page 255
Trinity - page 257
Corpus Christi - page 258
Sundays after Trinity - page 261
Time before Advent page 269

SANCTORAL CYCLE - pages 271-300

Requiem - page 301
Votive Masses - page 302

PREMISES OF THE FAITH - page 309

COME AND WORSHIP

PREFACE

This is not a Roman Catholic Missal. This Missal is intended for use within the Independent Sacramental Tradition, and the rites presented are those employed by the Autocephalous Catholic Church of Antioch: the parent body of which is the Catholic Apostolic Church of Antioch. Both of these churches are, by definition and in fact, Catholic: which is to say that they continue, validly, legitimately and verifiably, in historical and unbroken succession from the Apostles of Christ. They are thus living members and constituent parts of the One, Holy, Catholic and Apostolic Church. Likewise, by definition and in fact, because they are Independent, like other churches of the Independent Sacramental Tradition they are not in communion with the See of Rome. They are Catholic, but they are not *Roman* Catholic.

The contents of this Missal owe little to the rites of the Liberal Catholic Church, but instead draw largely upon the learning, traditions and texts of the mediaeval Church; while the influence of the Anglican Church will be apparent, not, indeed, in the sacramental thinking exemplified herein, but in the 'known-from-of-old' quality of a number of the prayers.

Archaic language has been avoided herein, with the exception of several well-known hymns and one version of the Lord's Prayer. The Missal has, therefore, a contemporary spirit, but without detriment to the beauty and mystery of the ageless truths it expresses.

The feast of the Immaculate Conception will not be found in this Missal; but the Assumption is celebrated, and the Blessed Lady Mary is revered as the holiest of the Saints, the Mother of our Lord. The mystical

PREFACE

implications of Mary's status as the Archetype of the Church and as the Mother of Jesus are not emphasised, but neither are they ignored; and the interpretation of these things is, rightly, left to individual conscience.

Each of the texts of the Ordinary of the Mass and of the Rite of Baptism given here is presented in five sections: these sections relating to the established mediaeval scheme of the Spiritual Life, as set forth by, among others, Saint Ambrose, Saint Augustine and Saint Bernard.

This Missal accords with the established principles and age-old definitions of the Catholic Faith, and with its apostolic traditions. The three creeds of the Universal Church – *Nicene, Apostles' and Athanasian* – are implicit herein and foundational hereto. A contemporary Affirmation of Faith, which is in harmony with these creeds, and which acknowledges the potential inherent in the interaction of the human with the divine, also has place here.

The theological understanding and definition of the sacraments, as presented herein, is consistent with that of the Council of Trent.

+Leon Roger Hunt
Presiding Bishop, ACCOA

Feast of the Assumption
August 2013

COME AND WORSHIP

THE LITURGICAL YEAR

TEMPORAL CYCLE

ADVENT

First Sunday of Advent - Violet
Second Sunday of Advent - Violet
Third Sunday of Advent - Violet
Fourth Sunday of Advent - Violet

Eve of the Nativity - Violet

NATIVITY

Feast of the Nativity - White or Gold
First Sunday of the Nativity - White
Second Sunday of the Nativity - White

EPIPHANY

Feast of the Epiphany (January 6) - White or Gold
First Sunday after Epiphany - White
Second Sunday after Epiphany - Green
Third Sunday after Epiphany - Green
Fourth Sunday after Epiphany - Green
Fifth Sunday after Epiphany - Green
Sixth Sunday after Epiphany - Green

TIME BEFORE LENT

Septuagesima - Green
Sexagesima - Green
Quinquagesima - Green

LITURGICAL YEAR

LENT

Ash Wednesday - Violet
First Sunday of Lent - Violet
Second Sunday of Lent - Violet
Third Sunday of Lent - Violet
Fourth Sunday of Lent - Violet
Fifth Sunday of Lent - Violet
Sixth Sunday of Lent (Palm Sunday) - Red, Violet
Monday in Holy Week - Violet
Tuesday in Holy Week - Violet
Wednesday in Holy Week - Violet
Maundy Thursday - White
Good Friday (Christ's Passion and Death) – Black, Violet
Holy Saturday (Vigil of the Resurrection) - Violet, White

EASTER

Feast of the Resurrection – White or Gold
Monday in Easter Week - White
Tuesday in Easter Week - White
Wednesday in Easter Week - White
Thursday in Easter Week - White
Friday in Easter Week - White
Saturday in Easter Week – White
Second Sunday of Easter – White
Third Sunday of Easter – White
Fourth Sunday of Easter – White
Fifth Sunday of Easter – White
Sixth Sunday of Easter – White
Holy Thursday (Feast of the Ascension) – White or Gold
Seventh Sunday of Easter – White

PENTECOST

Pentecost Sunday – Red

COME AND WORSHIP

TRINITY

Trinity Sunday - White or Gold

Thursday after Trinity Sunday (Corpus Christi) - White

SUNDAYS AFTER TRINITY

First Sunday after Trinity - Green
Second Sunday after Trinity - Green
Third Sunday after Trinity - Green
Fourth Sunday after Trinity - Green
Fifth Sunday after Trinity - Green
Sixth Sunday after Trinity - Green
Seventh Sunday after Trinity - Green
Eighth Sunday after Trinity - Green
Ninth Sunday after Trinity - Green
Tenth Sunday after Trinity - Green
Eleventh Sunday after Trinity - Green
Twelfth Sunday after Trinity - Green
Thirteenth Sunday after Trinity - Green
Fourteenth Sunday after Trinity - Green
Fifteenth Sunday after Trinity - Green
Sixteenth Sunday after Trinity - Green
Seventeenth Sunday after Trinity - Green
Eighteenth Sunday after Trinity - Green
Nineteenth Sunday after Trinity - Green
Twentieth Sunday after Trinity - Green
Twenty-first Sunday after Trinity - Green
Twenty-Second Sunday after Trinity - Green
Last Sunday after Trinity - Green

TIME BEFORE ADVENT

Fourth Sunday before Advent - Red
Third Sunday before Advent - Red
Second Sunday before Advent - Red
Christ the King (Sunday next before Advent) - White

LITURGICAL YEAR

SANCTORAL CYCLE

JANUARY

1 - The Naming of the Lord - White
2 - Basil the Great and Gregory of Nazianzus - White
6 - The Epiphany - White or Gold
8 - Gudula - White
13 - The Baptism of Christ
17 - Anthony of Egypt - White
25 - Conversion of St. Paul - White
28 - Thomas Aquinas - White

FEBRUARY

1 - Brigid of Kildare - White
2 - The Presentation - White
14 - Cyril and Methodius - White
23 - Polycarp, Martyr - Red

MARCH

1 - David of Wales - White
2 - Chad of Lichfield - White
17 - Patrick of Ireland - White
19 - Joseph of Nazareth - White
20 - Cuthbert - White
25 - The Annunciation - White or Gold

APRIL

21 - Anselm of Canterbury - White
23 - George of England, Martyr - Red
25 - Mark, Evangelist, Martyr - Red
29 - Catherine of Siena - White

MAY

1 - Phillip and James, Apostles - Red

COME AND WORSHIP

2 - Athanasius of Alexandria - White
14 - Matthias, Apostle, Martyr - Red
31 - The Visitation - White

JUNE

1 - Justin, Martyr - Red
9 - Columba of Iona - White
11 - Barnabas, Martyr - Red
22 - Alban, Martyr - Red
24 - Birth of John the Baptist - White
27 - Cyril of Alexandria - White
28 - Irenaeus - White
29 - Peter and Paul, Apostles, Martyrs - Red

JULY

3 - Thomas, Apostle, Martyr - Red
11 - Benedict of Nursia - White
22 - Mary Magdalene - White
25 - James, Apostle, Martyr - Red

AUGUST

6 - The Transfiguration - White or Gold
10 - Laurence, Martyr - Red
11 - Clare of Assisi - White
15 - The Assumption of Blessed Mary - White
20 - Bernard of Clairvaux - White
24 - Bartholomew, Apostle, Martyr - Red
28 - Augustine of Hippo - White
31 - Aidan of Lindisfarne - White

SEPTEMBER

3 - Gregory the Great - White
13 - John Chrysostom - White
14 - Holy Cross Day - Red
16 - Euphemia, Martyr - Red
17 - Hildegard of Bingen - White

LITURGICAL YEAR

21 - Matthew, Apostle, Martyr - Red
29 - Michael and All Angels - White
30 - Jerome - White

OCTOBER

4 - Francis of Assisi - White
12 - Symeon the New Theologian - White
13 - Edward, Confessor - White
15 - Teresa of Avila - White
17 - Ignatius of Antioch, Martyr - Red
18 - Luke, Evangelist, Martyr - Red
28 - Simon and Jude, Apostles, Martyrs - Red

NOVEMBER

1 - All Saints' Day - White
2 - All Souls' Day - Black
10 - Leo the Great - White
14 - Gregory Palamas - White
20 - Edmund, Martyr - Red
22 - Cecilia, Martyr - Red
30 - Andrew, Apostle, Martyr - Red

DECEMBER

7 - Ambrose of Milan - White
14 - John of the Cross - White
24 - Eve of the Nativity - Violet
25 - The Nativity - White or Gold
26 - Stephen, Proto-martyr - Red
27 - John, Apostle and Evangelist - White
28 - The Holy Innocents - Red

The Mass

COME AND WORSHIP

ASPERGES

The Preparation of the Place

The priest bows profoundly to the altar, then receives the aspergillum and purifies with Holy Water, sprinkling towards the altar (centre, right and left) and intoning:

Sprinkle me with hyssop, O Lord, and I shall be clean.
R. Wash me and I shall be whiter than snow.

The priest faces the nave, and purifies with Holy Water, sprinkling towards the nave (centre, right and left) and intoning:

Embrace me with your love, O God.
R. According to your great and loving kindness.

The priest resigns the aspergillum, faces the altar, and bows while saying:

Glory be to the Father and to the Son and to the Holy Spirit.
R. As it was in the beginning, is now, and ever shall be, world without end. Amen.

Sprinkle me with hyssop, O Lord, and I shall be clean.
R. Wash me and I shall be whiter than snow.

O Lord, pour forth your love upon us.
R. And grant us your salvation.

ASPERGES

Lord, hear our prayer.
R. And let our cry come before you.

The Lord be with you.
R. And also with you.

Let us pray.

The priest now prays for God to send his heavenly guardian-messenger:

O Lord, holy One, omnipotent and eternal God, hear our prayer, and in your goodness send your holy angel from heaven, to watch over, to cherish and to protect, to abide with and to defend, all who dwell in this house.
R. Amen.

COME AND WORSHIP

VIDI AQUAM

The Preparation of the Place

(Easter Sunday to Pentecost Sunday)

The priest bows profoundly to the altar, then receives the aspergillum and purifies with Holy Water, sprinkling towards the altar (centre, right and left) and intoning:

I saw water flowing from the right side of the temple, alleluia.
R. And all to whom that water came were saved, alleluia, alleluia!

The priest purifies with Holy Water, sprinkling towards the nave (centre, right and left) and intoning:

Give thanks to the Lord for the Lord is good.
R. The love of the Lord endures for ever.

The priest resigns the aspergillum, faces the altar, and bows while saying:

Glory be to the Father and to the Son and to the Holy Spirit.
R. As it was in the beginning, is now, and ever shall be, world without end. Amen.

I saw water flowing from the right side of the temple, alleluia.
R. And all to whom that water came were saved, alleluia, alleluia!

VIDI AQUAM

O Lord, pour forth your love upon us.
R. And grant us your salvation.

Lord, hear our prayer.
R. And let our cry come before you.

The Lord be with you.
R. And also with you.

Let us pray.

The priest now prays for God to send his heavenly guardian-messenger:

O Lord, holy One, omnipotent and eternal God, hear our prayer, and in your goodness send your holy angel from heaven, to watch over, to cherish and to protect, to abide with and to defend, all who dwell in this house.
R. Amen.

COME AND WORSHIP

ORDER OF MASS

(Rite 1)

1 - THE INSPIRING BREATH

INVOCATION

The priest kisses the altar; then all make the sign of the cross as the priest says:

In the name of the Father and of + the Son and of the Holy Spirit.
R. Amen.

GREETING

One of the following forms of greeting is given.

(1)

The light and peace of Christ be with you.
R. And also with you.

(2)

Grace be with you, and peace, from the One who is, who was, and who is to come; and from the seven spirits which are before the throne; and from Jesus Christ, who is the faithful witness, the firstborn from the dead and the prince of the kings of the earth.
R. Amen.

RITE 1

(3)

Peace be to all, and love with faith, from God the Father, and the Lord Jesus Christ.
R. Grace be with all who love our Lord Jesus Christ.

(4)

The Lord be with you.
R. And also with you.

(5)

I will go to the altar of God,
R. Even to the God of my joy and gladness.

Send forth your light and your truth:
R. Let them lead me, and bring me to your holy hill and to your tabernacles.

And I will go to the altar of God,
R. Even to the God of my joy and gladness.

The Lord be with you.
R. And also with you.

CONFESSION

To prepare ourselves to celebrate the holy mysteries, let us humbly and sincerely confess ours failings to almighty God: first in the silence and stillness of the heart, and then with prayerful voice.

COME AND WORSHIP

A period of silence for private recollection of failings is now observed, after which one of the following is said by all:

(1)

Gracious God, I come before you, trusting in your great and loving kindness.
I adore you.
My soul praises you and blesses your holy name.
For all my failings towards you, most loving Lord, towards my fellow human beings, and towards myself, I am truly repentant.
Hear me, O God of Truth.
I open my heart to you.
I welcome the outpouring of your healing light, and with the aid of your grace I will walk henceforth in the paths of righteousness.

(2)

Loving God,
Father, Son and Holy Spirit:
I have sinned against you in thought, word and deed;
I have not always loved you with all my heart;
I have not always loved my neighbour as myself.
For all my failings towards you, most gracious God, towards my fellow human beings and towards myself, both those failings which are known to me and those which are unrecognised, I am truly sorry.
Forgive me all that is past, I pray you, restore the beauty of your image within me, and lead me from darkness into your wonderful light.

RITE 1

(3)

I confess to almighty God,
the Father, the Son and the Holy Spirit,
that I have sinned in thought, word and deed,
through my own most grievous fault.
Wherefore I pray almighty God
to have mercy upon me,
to forgive me all my sins,
and to bring me to everlasting life.

ABSOLUTION

May the almighty and loving Lord, the God of all mercy, grant us + forgiveness and perfect remission of our sins, time for amendment of life, and the grace and comfort of the Holy Spirit.
R. Amen.

FIRST INCENSATION

If incense is to be used, the priest blesses it.

May you be blessed + by the one in whose honour you are to burn. Amen.

The priest censes the altar and is in turn censed.

INTROIT

The Introit is said or sung by all. (Further Introit verses are given on pages 91-103.)

Blessed be the Holy Trinity, the undivided

COME AND WORSHIP

Unity.
We will praise God for the loving-kindness that
is shown to us. O Lord, our Lord, how wonderful
is your name in all the earth.
Glory be to the Father and to the Son and to the
Holy Spirit.
As it was in the beginning, is now, and ever shall
be, world without end. Amen.
Blessed be the Holy Trinity, the undivided
Unity.

KYRIE

*One of the following forms of the Kyrie is now said or
sung.*

(1)

Lord, have mercy.
R. Lord, have mercy.
Christ, have mercy.
R. Christ, have mercy.
Lord, have mercy.
R. Lord, have mercy.

(2)

Lord, pour forth your love upon us.
R. Lord, have mercy.
Christ, embrace us with your love.
R. Christ, have mercy.
Lord, uplift us in your love.
R. Lord, have mercy.

RITE 1

(3)

Kyrie eleison.
R. Kyrie eleison.
Christe eleison.
R. Christe eleison.
Kyrie eleison.
R. Kyrie eleison.

GLORIA

The Gloria is used on all Sundays and principal Feasts, except during penitential seasons; but it is used during the evening mass of Maundy Thursday. It is omitted on Ferias, except those occurring in Eastertide. It is not used during Requiems. Neither is it used during votive masses, with, however, these exceptions: it is employed for votive masses of the Virgin Mary on Saturdays; it is used in votive masses of the angels; and it is used when a votive mass is said 'for grave cause'.

When used, the Gloria is said or sung by all present:

Glory be to God on high, and in earth peace to all of goodwill. We praise you, we bless you, we worship you, we glorify you, we give thanks to you for your great glory, O Lord God, heavenly King, God the Father almighty. O Lord, the only-begotten Son, Jesus Christ. O Lord God, Lamb of God, Son of the Father. You who take away the sins of the world: have mercy on us. You who take away the sins of the world: receive our prayer. You who sit at the right hand of God the Father: have mercy on us. For you alone are holy, you alone are the Lord, you alone are the

COME AND WORSHIP

**most high, Jesus Christ, with the + Holy Spirit in
the glory of God the Father. Amen.**

COLLECTS

The Lord be with you.
R. And also with you.

Let us pray.

*The priest offers the Collect(s) for the day, to which
those present respond:*

R. Amen.

RITE 1

2 - THE RECEIVING BODY

Pattern 1
For Sundays and Principal Feasts

EPISTLE

A reading from ......

At the conclusion:

This is the Word of the Lord.
R. Thanks be to God.

ACCLAMATION

This, or another text (as provided on pages 104-107), is said or sung by all:

God is light, and in him is no darkness at all.
Come, let us walk in the light of the Lord.

MUNDA COR MEUM

Priest or deacon says the following prayer quietly:

Cleanse my heart and my lips, almighty God, as you cleansed the lips of the prophet Isaiah with a burning ember; and in the abundance of your loving-kindness grant me such purity that I may fittingly proclaim your holy Gospel. Through Christ our Lord. Amen.

COME AND WORSHIP

The priest now says, as appropriate:

May the Lord be in my (your) heart and on my (your) lips, that I (you) may well and worthily proclaim his Gospel. Amen.

GOSPEL

The Lord be with you.
R. And also with you.

The priest signs the book of the Gospels with the cross; then, as the Gospel is announced, all sign the cross upon forehead, lips and breast.

A reading from the holy Gospel according to **N.**
R. Glory to you, O Lord.

At the conclusion of the Gospel:

This is the Gospel of the Lord.
R. Praise to you, O Christ.

THE ADDRESS

When given, the address is preceded and followed by the Invocation:
In the name of the Father,
and of + the Son,
and of the Holy Spirit.
Amen.

RITE 1

SPIRITUAL AFFIRMATIONS

These Affirmations, used on Sundays and principal Feasts, are said by all. Either of the forms following may be used.

(1)

We believe in God the Father, the fount of life and holiness, the creator and ruler of all things, infinite in wisdom, power and love, the source of all goodness, beauty and truth.

We believe in Jesus the Christ, God made manifest in the flesh, our example, our teacher, our liberator and our redeemer.

We believe in the Holy Spirit, the one who maintains and nourishes all of creation, who is ever present with us for guidance, for comfort, for purification, for strength and for inspiration.

We believe in the forgiveness of sins; our forgiveness of ourselves and of others, being the measure of our alignment with God's infinite love.

We believe that a life of prayer and unceasing spiritual endeavour avails the advancement of the soul and enriches the Christian pilgrimage.

We believe that the provision of loving service to others, in faithfulness to the example of our Lord Jesus Christ, is both a duty and a privilege.

We believe that the particular presence of God

COME AND WORSHIP

is personalised to every individual, and is the inmost light of the soul.

We believe that there is grace for every need, that every need is supplied, and that those who live in the nature of the Christ lack for nothing.

We believe that God is eternally revealed to us in the Holy Scriptures and in our souls, and that God's signature may be discerned in the loving works and noble endeavours of humankind, in the arts and sciences, and in the natural wonders of the universe.

We believe in the Church, the community of the sons and daughters of God, as a focus for worship and as a catalyst for spiritual growth.

We believe that truth, harmony and righteousness shall prevail, resulting in a dynamic quality of life, beginning here on Earth, and continuing throughout eternity.

(2)

There is one Body and One Spirit.
One Lord, one Faith, one Baptism.
One God and Parent of us all, who is above all, through all, and in all.

PRAYERS OF INTERCESSION

One of the following forms of Intercession is offered.

RITE 1

(1)

Let us pray to the Father, through Christ, in the power of the Holy Spirit.

Strengthen your holy catholic Church in the service of Christ, O Lord. Keep her in peace and unity, watch over her, and guide her; together with our bishop ......, all our clergy, and all true believers and professors of the catholic and apostolic faith.

Lord, hear us.
R. Lord, graciously hear us.

Bless all your people: those here present, and all who love and serve you throughout the world; remembering all those who are in any way afflicted, or distressed, in mind, body, or estate (especially ......).

Lord, hear us.
R. Lord, graciously hear us.

Other specific intercessions may be introduced at this point.

Remember those of our brothers and sisters who have gone before us from this world, signed with the seal of faith (especially ......). We pray you, Lord, to lead these, and all who rest in Christ, into the place of refreshment, light and peace.

Lord, hear us.
Lord, graciously hear us.

COME AND WORSHIP

Reverently calling to mind the blessed Lady Mary,
your holy apostles and martyrs Peter and Paul, (N
......) and all your glorious saints, who have been
the chosen vessels of your grace and lights of the
world in their several generations, we pray that
rejoicing in their company and following their
good examples we may be made partakers with
them of your heavenly kingdom.

Lord, hear us.
R. Lord, graciously hear us.

In the abundance of your loving-kindness, O Lord,
be pleased to receive the prayers of your people,
and graciously grant that those things which we
ask according to your holy will may effectually be
obtained, to the honour of your name and to the
setting forth of your glory; through Jesus Christ
our Lord.
R. Amen.

(2)

Let us pray to the Father, through Christ, in the
power of the Holy Spirit.

Remember, Lord, your one, holy, catholic and
apostolic Church, redeemed by the blood of your
Christ. Grant that it may be a holy temple
acceptable to you: show forth its unity; fill it with
all truth, and in all truth with all peace.

Lord, hear our prayer.
R. Graciously hear us, O Lord.

Inspire and strengthen our bishop ......, all our

RITE 1

clergy, and all true believers and professors of the catholic and apostolic faith.

Lord, hear our prayer.
R. Graciously hear us, O Lord.

Bless all your people, Lord, and guide them in the paths of righteousness, peace and love: those who are here present, and all who love and serve you throughout the world (especially ......).

Lord, hear our prayer.
R. Graciously hear us, O Lord.

Other specific intercessions may be introduced here.

Remember all those of our brothers and sisters who have died in the peace of Christ (especially ......). Lead them into the joyful Feast in the fullness of your presence, together with the Blessed Lady Mary, with your holy apostles Peter and Paul (with ......), and with the whole company of saints, for whom your friendship was life.

Lord, hear our prayer.
R. Graciously hear us, O Lord.

In the abundance of your loving-kindness, O Lord, be pleased to receive the prayers of your people, and graciously grant that those things which we ask according to your holy will may effectually be obtained, to the honour of your name and to the setting forth of your glory; through Jesus Christ our Lord.
R. Amen.

COME AND WORSHIP

2 - THE RECEIVING BODY

Pattern 2
For all other celebrations

EPISTLE

A reading from ......

At the conclusion:

This is the Word of the Lord.
R. Thanks be to God.

ACCLAMATION

This, or another text, (as provided on pages 104-107) is said or sung by all.

Great and marvelous are your deeds, Lord God almighty.
Just and true are your ways, King of the ages.
Who will not reverence you, O Lord, and glorify your name?
For you alone are holy.
All nations will come and worship before you,
for your righteous acts have been revealed.

GOSPEL

The Lord be with you.
R. And also with you.

RITE 1

The priest signs the book of the Gospels with the cross; then, as the Gospel is announced, all sign the cross upon forehead, lips and breast.

A reading from the holy Gospel according to **N.**
R. Glory to you, O Lord.

At the conclusion of the Gospel:

This is the Gospel of the Lord.
R. Praise to you, O Christ.

COME AND WORSHIP

3 - JUSTICE

OFFERTORY

The Offertory text (pages 121-123) is here read or sung.

The priest offers the bread:

Loving God, almighty and eternal One, source of all goodness, beauty and truth: with thankful hearts we offer you this bread, this gift of your earth, fashioned by your children. It will become for us the body of your Christ.
R. May our hunger be satisfied with the bread of heaven.

The priest pours wine into the chalice; and then a little blessed water, saying quietly:

By the + mystery signified in the mingling of this water and wine, grant us to share in the godhead of Christ, who humbled himself to share our humanity.

The priest offers the wine:

Loving God, almighty and eternal One, source of all goodness, beauty and truth: with thankful hearts we offer you this wine, this gift of your earth, fashioned by your children. It will become for us the blood of your Christ.
R. May our thirst be allayed with the cup of everlasting salvation.

RITE 1

SECOND INCENSATION

If incense is to be used it is now blessed.

Be pleased, O Lord, to + bless this incense and to accept its fragrance.

The priest censes the bread and wine, saying:

With your own blessing, Lord, let this incense rise before you, and bring down upon us your mercy.

The priest censes the altar, saying:

May my prayer rise to you as fragrant incense, O Lord, as an evening offering from my outstretched hands.

The priest returns the thurible to the minister, saying:

May the Lord kindle within us the fire of his love, and the flame of everlasting charity.

Celebrant, ministers and people are then censed in due order.

LAVABO

Washing the hands, the priest says quietly:

I will wash my hands among the innocent, O Lord, and go about your altar; the praise of you in my ears and all your wonders on my lips. Lord, I love the beauty of your house, the dwelling-place of your glory.

COME AND WORSHIP

ORATE

My friends, pray that my sacrifice and yours may be acceptable to God the Father almighty.
R. May the Lord receive the sacrifice at your hands, to the praise and glory of his name, for our good and the good of all his holy Church.

PRAYER OVER THE OFFERINGS

Almighty God, may this spiritual oblation which we make to you in memory of the passion, resurrection and ascension of our Lord Jesus Christ, and in union with which we offer and present to your divine majesty ourselves as a holy and living sacrifice, be a praise worthy of your majesty and a means of redemption for us; through Christ our Lord.
R. Amen.

RITE 1

4 - MERCY

(Sursum Corda, Preface, Sanctus, Form 1)

SURSUM CORDA

The Lord be with you.
R. And also with you.

Lift up your hearts.
R. We lift them to the Lord.

Let us give thanks to the Lord our God.
R. It is right to give God thanks and praise.

PREFACE

(Other prefaces are given on pages 108-119)

It is truly worthy and just, right and wholesome, to give you thanks and praise, O holy and eternal God: for in Jesus Christ you call us to glory and virtue, and bestow upon us all things that lead to fullness of life and sanctification. Therefore, we praise you, joining our voices with the celestial choirs and with all the faithful of every time and place who for ever sing to the glory of your name:

SANCTUS AND BENEDICTUS

All now say or sing:

COME AND WORSHIP

Holy, Holy, Holy, Lord God of Hosts,
heaven and earth are full of your glory.
Hosanna in the highest!
Blessed is he + who comes in the name of the
Lord.
Hosanna in the highest!

(Sursum Corda, Preface, Sanctus, Form 2)

SURSUM CORDA

May the Lord be with you.
R. And with you may he be also.

Lift your hearts unto the Lord.
R. To our God we have upraised them.

Let us give thanks to the Lord.
R. It is right to thank and praise him.

PREFACE

(Other prefaces are given on pages 108-119)

It is truly worthy and just, right and wholesome,
to give you thanks and praise, O holy and eternal
God: for in Jesus Christ you call us to glory and
virtue, and bestow upon us all things that lead to
fullness of life and sanctification. Therefore, we
praise you, joining our voices with the celestial
choirs and with all the faithful of every time and
place who for ever sing to the glory of your name:

35

RITE 1

SANCTUS AND BENEDICTUS

All now say or sing:

Holy, Holy, Holy Lord,
God of Power and Might:
Your great glory fills the worlds.
Glory in the highest!
Blessed is the one who comes,
in the Lord's name + Christos comes.
Hosanna in the highest!

EUCHARISTIC PRAYER

The celebrant kisses the altar.

Almighty and ever-living God, we worship you, and we give you thanks for your great glory. Holy are you, Father, and holy indeed, with your only-begotten Son and the Holy Spirit.

When we turned our hearts from you, you did not abandon us to the power of desolation: of your great mercy, and in the plenitude of your boundless love, you gave your only-begotten Son, our Saviour Jesus Christ, to suffer death upon the altar of the cross as the perfect and sufficient sacrifice for the sins of the whole world, and for the renewal of your creation.

Through him, O Father, in union with [*the blessed Lady Mary, with your holy apostles and martyrs Peter and Paul, (with ......) and with*] all your saints, we offer you this spiritual worship, this sacrifice of praise, celebrating this Eucharist in

COME AND WORSHIP

time and space in faithfulness to his saving command: acknowledging the one, eternal and transcendent sacrifice of the Lamb slain from the foundation of the world.

Most loving and gracious Father, look favourably upon these gifts of bread and wine, we pray you. Let your Holy and Life-giving Spirit rest upon them, to perfect, + bless and sanctify them, that they may become for us the body and blood of your dearly beloved Son, our Lord Jesus Christ.

On the day before he suffered he took bread, and after giving thanks to you he broke it, and gave it to his disciples, saying: Take this, all of you, and eat of it:

FOR THIS IS MY BODY.

In like manner he took the cup, and after he had given thanks he gave it to his disciples, saying: Take this, all of you and drink of it:

FOR THIS IS MY BLOOD
OF THE NEW AND EVERLASTING COVENANT
– THE MYSTERY OF FAITH –
WHICH IS SHED FOR YOU AND FOR MANY
FOR THE FORGIVENESS OF SINS.

As often as you do these things, you shall do them
in memory of me.

Heavenly Father, calling to mind Christ's wondrous incarnation, his blessed passion and precious death, his mighty resurrection and

RITE 1

glorious ascension, we offer you in thanksgiving this living bread and this saving cup. And we ask you, of your loving-kindness, O God, to grant that those who partake worthily of this sacrament may feed in truth upon the body and blood of Christ.

Wherefore, O Father, in this sacred banquet in which the memorial of Christ's love is renewed and the pledge of future glory given, grant us so to receive your Son's body and blood that we may be united with him in mystic communion, that we may abide in him and he in us; that we may be renewed in the life of grace; and that our unity with all your church may be deepened and strengthened.

Make us worthy of everlasting life, O Lord our God, and grant that with all your saints we may enjoy for ever the shining vision of your glory; through Christ our Lord.

Through him, with him, in him,
in the unity of the Holy Spirit,
all honour and glory are yours,
almighty Father,
now and for ever.

The people give their assent to the Eucharistic Prayer:

Amen.

COME AND WORSHIP

5 - GLORY

THE LORD'S PRAYER

Let us pray. In obedience to the command of our blessed Lord, and following the universal practice of his holy Church, let us say together:

One of the following forms of the Lord's Prayer is now said by all.

(1)

Our Father who art in heaven, hallowed be thy name; thy kingdom come, thy will be done on earth as it is in heaven. Give us this day our daily bread; and forgive us our trespasses, as we forgive those who trespass against us. And lead us not into temptation, but deliver us from evil. Amen.

(2)

Our Father in heaven, may your name be sanctified, may your kingdom come, may your will be done on earth as in heaven. Give us this day our daily bread, and forgive us our debts, as we forgive our debtors. And let us not enter into temptation, but deliver us from evil. Amen.

THE PEACE

Lord Jesus Christ, you said to your apostles, Peace

RITE 1

I leave with you, my peace I give unto you: look not upon our sins, but upon the faith of your church, and be pleased to grant her the peace and unity which are agreeable to your will.
R. Amen.

The peace of the Lord be with you always.
R. And also with you.

[Let us offer one another a sign of Christ's peace.]

FRACTION

The priest breaks the host in half over the paten; places the right hand portion on the paten, breaks a small piece from the left hand portion and places the left hand portion on the paten. Holding the knop of the chalice with the left hand, the priest drops the small fragment from the left-hand portion into the chalice, saying:

Christ our Passover is sacrificed for us.
R. Let us therefore keep the Feast.

AGNUS DEI

The Agnus Dei is said or sung by all.

O Lamb of God, you take away the sins of the world: have mercy on us.
O Lamb of God, you take away the sins of the world: have mercy on us.
O Lamb of God, you take away the sins of the world: grant us your peace.

COME AND WORSHIP

PRAYER BEFORE COMMUNION

Almighty God, our heavenly Father, we worship you in this hour with great tenderness of heart and purity of mind. Grant us, we pray you, that we may worthily receive the most precious body and blood of your Son Jesus Christ, and be fulfilled with every grace and heavenly benediction and made one with him.
R. Amen.

INVITATION TO COMMUNION

The priest then elevates paten and chalice, saying:

Behold the Lamb of God; behold him who takes away the sins of the world.

And all say:

Lord, I am not worthy to receive you, but only say the word and my soul shall be healed.

COMMUNION

The priest receives the host:

May the body of our Lord Jesus Christ preserve my soul in everlasting life. Amen.

The priest receives the chalice:

May the blood of our Lord Jesus Christ preserve my soul in everlasting life. Amen.

RITE 1

Clergy and servers receive, and then the faithful.

May the body of our Lord Jesus Christ preserve
your soul in everlasting life.
R. Amen.

May the blood of our Lord Jesus Christ preserve
your soul in everlasting life.
R. Amen.

THE ABLUTIONS

*The sacred vessels are purified. The paten is purified
above the chalice. Wine is poured into the chalice over
the priest's fingers; then wine and water are together
poured into the chalice over the priest's fingers; and
finally water is poured into the chalice over the
priest's fingers. The sacred vessels are covered.*

COMMUNION ADORATION

*The following verses of praise, or others, are now said
or sung. These may, if desired, be begun during the
Ablutions. Or silence may be observed or music played
during the Ablutions, preceding the Communion
Adoration.*

Amen. Praise and glory and wisdom and thanks
and honour and power and strength be to our God
for ever and ever. Amen.
**R. To him who sits on the throne and to the
Lamb be praise and honour and glory and
power, for ever and ever.**

COME AND WORSHIP

POSTCOMMUNION PRAYER

The Lord be with you.
R. And also with you.

Let us pray.

The following prayer, or another, is said:

Almighty God, may we, who in these holy mysteries have been refreshed with your heavenly gifts, be restored in newness of life; and may we glorify your name, not only with our lips but in our lives: by giving ourselves to your service, and by walking in your light all our days; through Christ our Lord.
R. Amen.

RESPONSORY

May the almighty Lord order our days and our times in his peace.
R. May the Lord grant us his peace and eternal life.

GREETING

The Lord be with you.
R. And also with you.

BLESSING

The priest kisses the altar, and then gives the blessing.

RITE 1

May almighty God bless you: the Father, the +
Son, and the Holy Spirit.
R. Amen.

DISMISSAL

(1)

The Rite is ended, go in peace.
R. Thanks be to God.

(2)

Go forth in the Light of Christ.
R. Thanks be to God.

(3)

Go in peace to love and serve the Lord.
R. Thanks be to God.

COME AND WORSHIP

ORDER OF MASS

(Rite 2)

1 - THE INSPIRING BREATH

INVOCATION

All make the sign of the cross as the priest says:

In the name of the Father and of + the Son and of
the Holy Spirit.
R. Amen.

ANTHEM
I will go to the altar of God.
R. Even to the God of my joy and gladness.

PSALM.
Judge me, O God, and defend my cause against an
ungodly nation. Deliver me from the deceitful and
wicked man.
**R. For you, O God, are my strength. Why do you
cast me from you? Why do I go sorrowfully while
the enemy oppresses me?**
Send forth your light and your truth, that they
may lead me and bring me to your holy hill and to
your tabernacle.
**R. And I will go to the altar of God, even to the
God of my joy and gladness.**
I will proclaim you upon the harp, O God my God!
Why are you sad, O my soul, why are you

RITE 2

disquieted within me?
R. Hope in God, for I shall yet praise him, who is the health of my countenance and my God.
Glory be to the Father and to the Son and to the Holy Spirit.
R. As it was in the beginning, is now, and ever shall be, world without end. Amen.

ANTHEM.
I will go to the altar of God.
R. Even to the God of my joy and gladness.

CONFESSION

Our + help is in the name of the Lord.
R. Who made heaven and earth.

A period of silence for private recollection of failings is now observed, after which one of the following is said by all present:

(1)

Gracious God, I come before you, trusting in your great and loving kindness.
I adore you.
My soul praises you and blesses your holy name.
For all my failings towards you, most loving Lord, towards my fellow human beings, and towards myself, I am truly repentant.
Hear me, O God of Truth.
I open my heart to you.
I welcome the outpouring of your healing light, and with the aid of your grace I will walk henceforth in the paths of righteousness.

COME AND WORSHIP

(2)

Loving God,
Father, Son and Holy Spirit:
I have sinned against you in thought, word and
deed;
I have not always loved you with all my heart;
I have not always loved my neighbour as myself.
For all my failings towards you, most gracious
God, towards my fellow human beings and
towards myself, both those failings which are
known to me and those which are unrecognised,
I am truly sorry.
Forgive me all that is past, I pray you, restore
the beauty of your image within me, and lead
me from darkness into your wonderful light.

(3)

I confess to almighty God,
the Father, the Son and the Holy Spirit,
that I have sinned in thought, word and deed,
through my own most grievous fault.
Wherefore I pray almighty God
to have mercy upon me,
to forgive me all my sins,
and to bring me to everlasting life.

ABSOLUTION

May the almighty and loving Lord, the God of all
mercy, grant us + forgiveness and perfect
remission of our sins, time for amendment of life,
and the grace and comfort of the Holy Spirit.
R. Amen.

RITE 2

APPROACH

Turn to us, O God, and give us life.
R. And your people will rejoice in you.
O Lord, pour forth your love upon us.
R. And grant us your salvation.
Lord, hear our prayer.
R. And let our cry come before you.

The Lord be with you.
R. And also with you.

Let us pray.

The priest approaches the altar, and says quietly:

Fill us with the dew of your loving-kindness, O God, that our hearts and minds may be purified and uplifted, and that we may worthily enter your Holy of Holies to minister before you in righteousness and innocence. Through Christ our Lord. Amen.

The priest kisses the altar.

INCENSATION

The priest blesses incense.

May you be blessed + by the one in whose honour you are to burn. Amen.

The priest censes the altar and is in turn censed.

COME AND WORSHIP

INTROIT

The Introit is said or sung by all. (Further Introit verses are given on pages 91-103)

Blessed be the Holy Trinity, the undivided Unity.
We will praise God for the loving-kindness that is shown to us. O Lord, our Lord, how wonderful is your name in all the earth.
Glory be to the Father and to the Son and to the Holy Spirit. As it was in the beginning, is now, and ever shall be, world without end. Amen.
Blessed be the Holy Trinity, the undivided Unity.

KYRIE

Kyrie eleison.
R. Kyrie eleison.
Kyrie eleison.

R. Christe eleison.
Christe eleison.
R. Christe eleison.

Kyrie eleison.
R. Kyrie eleison.
Kyrie eleison.

GLORIA

The Gloria is used on all Sundays and principal Feasts, except during penitential seasons; but it is used during

49

RITE 2

the evening mass of Maundy Thursday. It is omitted on Ferias, except those occurring in Eastertide. It is not used during Requiems. Neither is it used during votive masses, with, however, these exceptions: it is employed for votive masses of the Virgin Mary on Saturdays; it is used in votive masses of the angels; and it is used when a votive mass is 'for grave cause'.

When used, the Gloria is said or sung by all present:

Glory be to God on high, and in earth peace to all of goodwill. We praise you, we bless you, we worship you, we glorify you, we give thanks to you for your great glory, O Lord God, heavenly King, God the Father almighty. O Lord, the only-begotten Son, Jesus Christ. O Lord God, Lamb of God, Son of the Father. You who take away the sins of the world: have mercy on us. You who take away the sins of the world: receive our prayer. You who sit at the right hand of God the Father: have mercy on us. For you alone are holy, you alone are the Lord, you alone are the most high, Jesus Christ, with the + Holy Spirit in the glory of God the Father. Amen.

COLLECT

The Lord be with you.
R. And also with you.

Let us pray.

The priest reads the Collect(s) for the day, and all respond:

R. Amen.

COME AND WORSHIP

2 - THE RECEIVING BODY

THE EPISTLE

A reading from ......

At the conclusion:

This is the Word of the Lord.
R. Thanks be to God.

ACCLAMATION

This, or another text (as provided on pages 104-107), may be said or sung.

Great and marvelous are your deeds, Lord God almighty.
Just and true are your ways, King of the ages.
Who will not reverence you, O Lord, and glorify your name?
For you alone are holy.
All nations will come and worship before you,
for your righteous acts have been revealed.

MUNDA COR MEUM

The priest, or the deacon, says the following prayer quietly:

Cleanse my heart and my lips, almighty God, as you cleansed the lips of the prophet Isaiah with a

RITE 2

burning ember; and in the abundance of your loving-kindness grant me such purity that I may fittingly proclaim your holy Gospel. Through Christ our Lord. Amen.

The priest now says, as appropriate:

May the Lord be in my (your) heart and on my (your) lips, that I (you) may well and worthily proclaim his Gospel. Amen.

GOSPEL

The Lord be with you.
R. And also with you.

The priest signs the book of the Gospels with the cross; then, as the Gospel is announced, all sign the cross upon forehead, lips and breast.

A reading from the holy Gospel according to **N.**
R. Glory to you, O Lord.

At the conclusion of the Gospel:

This is the Gospel of the Lord.
R. Praise to you, O Christ.

THE ADDRESS

When given, the address is preceded and followed by the Invocation:
In the name of the Father,
and of + the Son,
and of the Holy Spirit.
Amen.

COME AND WORSHIP

SPIRITUAL AFFIRMATIONS

These Affirmations, used on Sundays and principal Feasts, are said by all. Either of the forms following may be used.

(1)

We believe in God the Father, the fount of life and holiness, the creator and ruler of all things, infinite in wisdom, power and love, the source of all goodness, beauty and truth.

We believe in Jesus the Christ, God made manifest in the flesh, our example, our teacher, our liberator and our redeemer.

We believe in the Holy Spirit, the one who maintains and nourishes all of creation, who is ever present with us for guidance, for comfort, for purification, for strength and for inspiration.

We believe in the forgiveness of sins; our forgiveness of ourselves and of others, being the measure of our alignment with God's infinite love.

We believe that a life of prayer and unceasing spiritual endeavour avails the advancement of the soul and enriches the Christian pilgrimage.

We believe that the provision of loving service to others, in faithfulness to the example of our Lord Jesus Christ, is both a duty and a privilege.

We believe that the particular presence of God

RITE 2

is personalised to every individual, and is the inmost light of the soul.

We believe that there is grace for every need, that every need is supplied, and that those who live in the nature of the Christ lack for nothing.

We believe that God is eternally revealed to us in the Holy Scriptures and in our souls, and that God's signature may be discerned in the loving works and noble endeavours of humankind, in the arts and sciences, and in the natural wonders of the universe.

We believe in the Church, the community of the sons and daughters of God, as a focus for worship and as a catalyst for spiritual growth.

We believe that truth, harmony and righteousness shall prevail, resulting in a dynamic quality of life, beginning here on Earth, and continuing throughout eternity.

(2)

There is one Body and One Spirit.
One Lord, one Faith, one Baptism.
One God and Parent of us all, who is above all, through all, and in all.

COME AND WORSHIP

3 - JUSTICE

OFFERTORY

The Offertory text following, or another (as provided on pages 121-123), is read or sung.

I am come that you might have life, and that you might have it more abundantly.

The priest offers the bread:

Accept, O Holy Father, almighty and eternal God, this immaculate oblation which we make to you with thankful hearts. May it bring us salvation, that we may attain to everlasting life. Amen.

The priest pours wine into the chalice; and then blessed water, saying quietly:

O God + who in creating us wonderfully exalted our nature, and yet more wonderfully established it anew: by the mystery signified in the mingling of this water and wine grant us to share in the godhead of him who deigned to share our humanity, Jesus Christ, your Son, our Lord. Amen.

The priest offers the wine:

We offer you the cup of salvation, Lord, and we ask of your loving-kindness that it may ascend with a sweet fragrance before your divine majesty for our salvation and for that of the whole world. Amen.

RITE 2

SECOND INCENSATION

Incense is now blessed.

May the Lord be pleased to bless + this incense and to accept its fragrance. Through Christ our Lord. Amen.

The priest censes the bread and wine, saying:

With your own blessing, Lord, let this incense rise before you, and bring down upon us your mercy.

The priest censes the altar, saying:

May my prayer rise up to you like fragrant incense, Lord, like an evening offering from my outstretched hands.

The priest returns the thurible to the minister, saying:

May the Lord kindle within us the fire of his love, and the flame of everlasting charity.

Celebrant, ministers and people are then censed in due order.

LAVABO

I will wash my hands among the innocent, O Lord, and go about your altar; the praise of you in my ears and all your wonders on my lips. Lord, I love the beauty of your house, the dwelling-place of your glory. I will praise you, Lord, in the gatherings of your people. Glory be to the Father, and to the Son, and to the Holy Spirit. As it was in the beginning, is now, and ever shall be, world without end. Amen.

COME AND WORSHIP

ORATE

My friends, pray that my sacrifice and yours may be acceptable to God the Father almighty.
R. May the Lord receive the sacrifice at your hands, to the praise and glory of his name, for our good and the good of all his holy Church.

PRAYER OVER THE OFFERINGS

Almighty God, may this spiritual oblation which we make to you in memory of the passion, resurrection and ascension of our Lord Jesus Christ, in union with which we offer and present to your divine majesty ourselves, as a holy and living sacrifice, be a praise worthy of your majesty and a means of redemption for us. Through Christ our Lord.
R. Amen.

RITE 2

4 - MERCY

SURSUM CORDA

The Lord be with you.
R. And also with you.

Lift up your hearts.
R. We lift them to the Lord.

Let us give thanks to the Lord our God.
R. It is right to give him thanks and praise.

PREFACE

(Other Prefaces are given on pages 108-119)

It is truly worthy and just, right and wholesome, to give you thanks and praise, O holy and eternal God: for in Jesus Christ you call us to glory and virtue, and bestow upon us all things that lead to fullness of life and sanctification. Therefore, we praise you, joining our voices with the celestial choirs and with all the faithful of every time and place who for ever sing to the glory of your name:

SANCTUS AND BENEDICTUS

Holy, Holy, Holy, Lord God of Hosts, heaven and earth are full of your glory. Hosanna in the highest!

COME AND WORSHIP

Blessed is he + who comes in the name of the Lord.
Hosanna in the highest!

THE EUCHARISTIC PRAYER

The priest kisses the altar.

Most loving Father, we your servants pray you, through Jesus Christ your Son our Lord, to receive and bless these gifts, these holy things we owe to you, these sacred, unblemished offerings.

We offer them for your holy catholic Church, that you may be pleased to keep her in peace and unity, to watch over her, and to guide her, together with our bishop ......, all our clergy, and all true believers and professors of the catholic and apostolic faith.

We offer them for your entire people: those here present, and all who love and serve you throughout the world (remembering especially ......).

And we offer them for all your children who have gone before us from this world, signed with the seal of faith (especially ......). We pray you, Lord, to lead these, and all who rest in Christ, into the place of refreshment, light and peace.

United in one sacred fellowship we reverently call to mind, first, the holy Lady Mary, mother of our God and Lord Jesus Christ, and then your blessed apostles and martyrs Peter and Paul, and all your

RITE 2

glorious saints, who have been the chosen vessels of your grace and lights of the world in their several generations; and we pray that rejoicing in their company and following their good examples, we may be made partakers with them of your heavenly kingdom.

This, then, O Lord, is the offering that we, the servants of your altar, together with your whole household, make to you. Be pleased, O God, to look upon it and to accept it, and with your Holy and Life-giving Spirit to + bless and sanctify it, that it may become for us the body and blood of your dearly beloved Son, our Lord Jesus Christ.

On the day before he suffered he took bread, and after giving thanks to you he broke it, and gave it to his disciples, saying: Take this, all of you, and eat of it:

FOR THIS IS MY BODY.

In like manner he took the cup, and after he had given thanks he gave it to his disciples, saying: Take this, all of you, and drink of it:

FOR THIS IS MY BLOOD
OF THE NEW AND EVERLASTING COVENANT
– THE MYSTERY OF FAITH –
WHICH IS SHED FOR YOU AND FOR MANY
FOR THE FORGIVENESS OF SINS.

As often as you do these things, you shall do them in memory of me.

COME AND WORSHIP

Wherefore, O Lord and heavenly Father, we, your humble servants, and with us all your holy people, bearing in mind the ineffable sacrifice of your Son, the mystery of his wondrous incarnation, his blessed passion and precious death, his mighty resurrection and glorious ascension, offer to your sovereign majesty, out of the gifts you have bestowed upon us, this pure, holy and immaculate host: the holy bread of life everlasting and the chalice of eternal salvation.

And humbly we pray you, almighty God, that you would command your holy angel to bear these things to your altar on high, in the sight of your divine majesty, so that those of us who shall have received your Son's most sacred body and blood by partaking of the altar here, may be filled with every grace and heavenly benediction.

Make us worthy of everlasting life, O Lord our God, and grant that with all your saints we may enjoy for ever the shining vision of your glory; through Christ our Lord.

Through him, with him, in him,
in the unity of the Holy Spirit,
all honour and glory are yours,
almighty Father,
Now and for ever.

All present give their assent to the Eucharistic Prayer:

Amen.

RITE 2

5 - GLORY

THE LORD'S PRAYER

Let us pray. In obedience to the command of our blessed Lord, and following the universal practice of his holy Church, let us say:

Our Father who art in heaven, hallowed be thy name; thy kingdom come, thy will be done on earth as it is in heaven. Give us this day our daily bread; and forgive us our trespasses, as we forgive those who trespass against us. And lead us not into temptation, but deliver us from evil. Amen.

THE PEACE

Lord Jesus Christ, you said to your apostles, Peace I leave with you, my peace I give to you: look not upon our sins, but upon the faith of your church, and be pleased to grant her the peace and unity which are agreeable to your will.
R. Amen.

The peace of the Lord be with you always.
R. And also with you.

Let us offer one another a sign of Christ's Peace.

The Peace is exchanged according to local custom.

COME AND WORSHIP

FRACTION

The priest breaks the host in half over the paten; he places the right hand portion on the paten, and breaks a small piece from the left hand portion and places the left hand portion on the paten. Holding the knop of the chalice with his left hand, he drops the small fragment from the left-hand portion into the chalice, saying:

May this commixture and consecration of the body and blood of our Lord Jesus Christ be for us who receive it a medicine for everlasting life.

AGNUS DEI

The Agnus Dei is said or sung by all.

**O Lamb of God, you take away the sins of the world: have mercy on us.
O Lamb of God, you take away the sins of the world: have mercy on us.
O Lamb of God, you take away the sins of the world: grant us your peace.**

PRAYER BEFORE COMMUNION

O Son of God, in this sacred banquet in which the memorial of your love is renewed and the pledge of future glory given, grant us so to receive your body and blood that we may be united with you in mystic communion, that we may abide in you and you in us; that we may be renewed in the life of grace; and that our unity with all your church may be deepened and strengthened.
R. Amen.

RITE 2

INVITATION TO COMMUNION

The priest then elevates paten and chalice, saying:

Holy things for the holy!

And all present proclaim:

**Jesus Christ is holy.
Jesus Christ is Lord.
To the glory of God the Father.**

COMMUNION

The priest receives the body of Christ:

May the body of our Lord Jesus Christ preserve my soul in everlasting life. Amen.

The priest receives the blood of Christ:

May the blood of our Lord Jesus Christ preserve my soul in everlasting life. Amen.

The priest administers to clergy and servers, and then to the people.

May the body of our Lord Jesus Christ preserve your soul in everlasting life.
R. Amen.

May the blood of our Lord Jesus Christ preserve your soul in everlasting life.
R. Amen.

COME AND WORSHIP

THE ABLUTIONS

The sacred vessels are purified. The paten is purified above the chalice. Wine is poured into the chalice over the priest's fingers; then wine and water are together poured into the chalice over the priest's fingers; and finally water is poured into the chalice over the priest's fingers. The sacred vessels are covered.

COMMUNION ADORATION

The following verses of praise, or others, are now said or sung. These may, if desired, be begun during the Ablutions. Or silence may be observed or music played during the Ablutions, preceding the Communion Adoration.

Amen. Praise and glory and wisdom and thanks and honour and power and strength be to our God for ever and ever. Amen.
R. To him who sits on the throne and to the Lamb be praise and honour and glory and power, for ever and ever.

POSTCOMMUNION PRAYER

The Lord be with you.
R. And also with you.

Let us pray.

The following prayer, or another, is now said.

Almighty God, may we, who in these holy mysteries have been refreshed with your heavenly

RITE 2

gifts, be restored in newness of life; and may we glorify your name, not only with our lips but in our lives: by giving ourselves to your service, and by walking in your light all our days; through Christ our Lord.
R. Amen.

RESPONSORY

May the almighty Lord order our days and our times in his peace.
R. May the Lord grant us his peace and eternal life.

GREETING

The Lord be with you.
R. And also with you.

DISMISSAL

(1)

The Rite is ended. Go in peace.
R. Thanks be to God.

(2)

When a procession follows Mass, the conclusion is:

Let us bless the Lord.
R. Thanks be to God.

COME AND WORSHIP

(3)

For Requiem Mass, the conclusion is:

May the souls of the faithful departed, through the mercy of God, rest in peace.
R. Amen.

BLESSING

The priest kisses the altar; then extends, raises and joins hands, bringing them to repose upon the chest. The priest says 'May almighty God bless you', and then gives the blessing with the right hand, the left hand remaining upon the chest, while saying, 'the Father, the Son, and the Holy Spirit.'

May almighty God bless you: the Father, + the Son, and the Holy Spirit.
R. Amen.

APOSTOLIC BLESSING

Blessed be the name of the Lord.
R. From this time forth and throughout all ages.
Our + help is in the name of the Lord.
R. Who made heaven and earth.
May almighty God bless you: the + Father, and the + Son, and the + Holy Spirit.
R. Amen.

RITE 3

ORDER OF MASS

(Rite 3)

1 - THE INSPIRING BREATH

INVOCATION

All make the sign of the cross as the priest says:

In the name of the Father and of + the Son and of the Holy Spirit.
R. Amen.

ANTHEM
I will go to the altar of God.
R. Even to the God of my joy and gladness.

PSALM.
Judge me, O God, and defend my cause against an ungodly nation. Deliver me from the deceitful and wicked man.
R. For you, O God, are my strength. Why do you cast me from you? Why do I go sorrowfully while the enemy oppresses me?
Send forth your light and your truth, that they may lead me and bring me to your holy hill and to your tabernacle.
R. And I will go to the altar of God, even to the God of my joy and gladness.
I will proclaim you upon the harp, O God my God! Why are you sad, O my soul, why are you

COME AND WORSHIP

disquieted within me?
**R. Hope in God, for I shall yet praise him, who is
the health of my countenance and my God.**
Glory be to the Father and to the Son and to the
Holy Spirit.
**R. As it was in the beginning, is now, and ever
shall be, world without end. Amen.**

ANTHEM.
I will go to the altar of God.
R. Even to the God of my joy and gladness.

CONFESSION

Our + help is in the name of the Lord.
R. Who made heaven and earth.

*A period of silence for private recollection of failings
is now observed, after which one of the following is
said by all present:*

(1)

Gracious God, I come before you, trusting in
your great and loving kindness.
I adore you.
My soul praises you and blesses your holy name.
For all my failings towards you, most loving
Lord, towards my fellow human beings, and
towards myself, I am truly repentant.
Hear me, O God of Truth.
I open my heart to you.
I welcome the outpouring of your healing light,
and with the aid of your grace I will walk
henceforth in the paths of righteousness.

69

RITE 3

(2)

Loving God,
Father, Son and Holy Spirit:
I have sinned against you in thought, word and deed;
I have not always loved you with all my heart;
I have not always loved my neighbour as myself.
For all my failings towards you, most gracious God, towards my fellow human beings and towards myself, both those failings which are known to me and those which are unrecognised, I am truly sorry.
Forgive me all that is past, I pray you, restore the beauty of your image within me, and lead me from darkness into your wonderful light.

(3)

I confess to almighty God,
the Father, the Son and the Holy Spirit,
that I have sinned in thought, word and deed,
through my own most grievous fault.
Wherefore I pray almighty God
to have mercy upon me,
to forgive me all my sins,
and to bring me to everlasting life.

ABSOLUTION

May the almighty and loving Lord, the God of all mercy, grant us + forgiveness and perfect remission of our sins, time for amendment of life, and the grace and comfort of the Holy Spirit.
R. Amen.

COME AND WORSHIP

APPROACH

Turn to us, O God, and give us life.
R. And your people will rejoice in you.

O Lord, pour forth your love upon us.
R. And grant us your salvation.

Lord, hear our prayer.
R. And let our cry come before you.

The Lord be with you.
R. And also with you.

Let us pray.

The priest approaches the altar, and says quietly:

Fill us with the dew of your loving-kindness, O God, that our hearts and minds may be purified and uplifted, and that we may worthily enter your Holy of Holies to minister before you in righteousness and innocence. Through Christ our Lord. Amen.

The priest kisses the altar.

FIRST INCENSATION

The priest blesses incense.

May you be blessed + by the one in whose honour you are to burn. Amen.

The priest censes the altar and is in turn censed.

RITE 3

INTROIT

The Introit verses are said or sung by all. (Further Introit verses are given on pages 91-103)

Blessed be the Holy Trinity, the undivided Unity.
We will praise God for the loving-kindness that is shown to us. O Lord, our Lord, how wonderful is your name in all the earth.
Glory be to the Father and to the Son and to the Holy Spirit. As it was in the beginning, is now, and ever shall be, world without end. Amen.
Blessed be the Holy Trinity, the undivided Unity.

KYRIE

Kyrie eleison.
R. Kyrie eleison.
Kyrie eleison.

R. Christe eleison.
Christe eleison.
R. Christe eleison.

Kyrie eleison.
R. Kyrie eleison.
Kyrie eleison.

GLORIA

The Gloria is used on all Sundays and principal Feasts, except during penitential seasons; but it is used during the evening mass of Maundy Thursday. It is omitted on

COME AND WORSHIP

Ferias, except those occurring in Eastertide. It is not used during Requiems. Neither is it used during votive masses, with, however, these exceptions: it is employed for votive masses of the Virgin Mary on Saturdays; it is used in votive masses of the angels; and it is used when a votive mass is 'for grave cause'.

When used, the Gloria is said or sung by all present:

Glory be to God on high, and in earth peace to all of goodwill. We praise you, we bless you, we worship you, we glorify you, we give thanks to you for your great glory, O Lord God, heavenly King, God the Father almighty. O Lord, the only-begotten Son, Jesus Christ. O Lord God, Lamb of God, Son of the Father. You who take away the sins of the world: have mercy on us. You who take away the sins of the world: receive our prayer. You who sit at the right hand of God the Father: have mercy on us. For you alone are holy, you alone are the Lord, you alone are the most high, Jesus Christ, with the + Holy Spirit in the glory of God the Father. Amen.

COLLECT

The Lord be with you.
R. And also with you.

Let us pray.

The priest reads the Collect(s) for the day, to which the response is:

R. Amen.

RITE 3

2 - THE RECEIVING BODY

EPISTLE

A reading from ......

At the conclusion of the Epistle:

This is the Word of the Lord.
R. Thanks be to God.

ACCLAMATION

This, or another text (as provided on pages 104-107), may be said or sung.

**Great and marvelous are your deeds, Lord God almighty.
Just and true are your ways, King of the ages.
Who will not reverence you, O Lord, and glorify your name?
For you alone are holy.
All nations will come and worship before you,
for your righteous acts have been revealed.**

MUNDA COR MEUM

The priest, or the deacon, says the following prayer quietly:

Cleanse my heart and my lips, almighty God, as you cleansed the lips of the prophet Isaiah with a burning ember; and in the abundance of your

COME AND WORSHIP

loving-kindness grant me such purity that I may fittingly proclaim your holy Gospel. Through Christ our Lord. Amen.

The priest now says, as appropriate:

May the Lord be in my (your) heart and on my (your) lips, that I (you) may well and worthily proclaim his Gospel. Amen.

GOSPEL

The Lord be with you.
R. And also with you.

The priest signs the book of the Gospels with the cross; then, as the Gospel is announced, all sign the cross upon forehead, lips and breast.

A reading from the holy Gospel according to **N.**
R. Glory to you, O Lord.

At the conclusion of the Gospel:

This is the Gospel of the Lord.
R. Praise to you, O Christ.

THE ADDRESS

When given, the address is preceded and followed by the Invocation:
In the name of the Father,
and of + the Son,
and of the Holy Spirit.
Amen.

RITE 3

SPIRITUAL AFFIRMATIONS

These Affirmations, used on Sundays and principal Feasts, are said by all. Any of the forms following may be used.

(1)

We believe in God the Father, the fount of life and holiness, the creator and ruler of all things, infinite in wisdom, power and love, the source of all goodness, beauty and truth.

We believe in Jesus the Christ, God made manifest in the flesh, our example, our teacher, our liberator and our redeemer.

We believe in the Holy Spirit, the one who maintains and nourishes all of creation, who is ever present with us for guidance, for comfort, for purification, for strength and for inspiration.

We believe in the forgiveness of sins; our forgiveness of ourselves and of others, being the measure of our alignment with God's infinite love.

We believe that a life of prayer and unceasing spiritual endeavour avails the advancement of the soul and enriches the Christian pilgrimage.

We believe that the provision of loving service to others, in faithfulness to the example of our Lord Jesus Christ, is both a duty and a privilege.

We believe that the particular presence of God

COME AND WORSHIP

is personalised to every individual, and is the inmost light of the soul.

We believe that there is grace for every need, that every need is supplied, and that those who live in the nature of the Christ lack for nothing.

We believe that God is eternally revealed to us in the Holy Scriptures and in our souls, and that God's signature may be discerned in the loving works and noble endeavours of humankind, in the arts and sciences, and in the natural wonders of the universe.

We believe in the Church, the community of the sons and daughters of God, as a focus for worship and as a catalyst for spiritual growth.

We believe that truth, harmony and righteousness shall prevail, resulting in a dynamic quality of life, beginning here on Earth, and continuing throughout eternity.

(2)

There is one Body and One Spirit.
One Lord, one Faith, one Baptism.
One God and parent of us all, who is above all, through all, and in all.

(3)

We believe in one God, the Father almighty, maker of heaven and earth, and of all things visible and invisible.

RITE 3

We believe in one Lord, Jesus Christ, the only begotten Son of God, born of the Father before all ages. God from God, Light from Light, true God from true God, begotten not made, of one substance with the Father. Through him all things were made. For us and for our salvation he came down from heaven. By the power of the Holy Spirit he became incarnate from the Virgin Mary, and was made man. He was crucified for us under Pontius Pilate. He suffered and was buried. On the third day he rose again according to the scriptures. He ascended into heaven and is seated at the right hand of the Father. He will come again in glory to judge both the living and the dead, and his kingdom shall have no end.

We believe in the Holy Spirit, the Lord and giver of life, who proceeds from the Father and the Son, who together with the Father and the Son is worshipped and glorified, who has spoken through the prophets. We believe in one, holy, catholic and apostolic Church. We acknowledge one baptism for the remission of sins. And we look for the resurrection of the dead, and the life of the world to come. Amen.

COME AND WORSHIP

3 - JUSTICE

OFFERTORY

The following Offertory text, or another (as given on pages 121-123), is here read or sung.

Melchizedek king of Salem, brought forth bread and wine; and he was the priest of the most high God.

The priest offers the bread:

Accept, O Holy Father, almighty and eternal God, this immaculate oblation which we make to you with thankful hearts. May it bring us salvation, that we may attain to everlasting life. Amen. +

The priest pours wine into the chalice; and then blessed water, saying quietly:

O God + who in creating us wonderfully exalted our nature, and yet more wonderfully established it anew: by the mystery signified in the mingling of this water and wine grant us to share in the godhead of him who deigned to share our humanity, Jesus Christ, your Son, our Lord. Amen.

The priest offers the wine:

We offer you the cup of salvation, Lord, and we ask of your loving-kindness that it may ascend with a sweet fragrance before your divine majesty for our salvation and for that of the whole world. Amen. +

RITE 3

The priest bows, saying:

May we who are reverent in spirit and pure in heart find favour with you, Lord, and may our sacrifice be so offered before you this day that it may please you, Lord our God.

Standing upright, the priest solemnly invokes the Holy Spirit:

Come, O Sanctifier, almighty and ever-living God, and + bless this sacrifice made ready for your holy name.

SECOND INCENSATION

Incense is now blessed.

May the Lord be pleased to + bless this incense and to accept its fragrance. Through Christ our Lord. Amen.

The priest censes the bread and wine, saying:

With your own + blessing, Lord, let this incense rise before you, and bring down upon us your mercy.

The priest censes the altar, saying:

May my prayer rise up to you like fragrant incense, Lord, like an evening offering from my outstretched hands.

The priest returns the thurible to the minister, saying:
May the Lord kindle within us the fire of his love, and the flame of everlasting charity.

COME AND WORSHIP

Celebrant, ministers and people are then censed in due order.

LAVABO

I will wash my hands among the innocent, O Lord, and go about your altar; the praise of you in my ears and all your wonders on my lips. Lord, I love the beauty of your house, the dwelling-place of your glory. I will praise you, Lord, in the gatherings of your people. Glory be to the Father, and to the Son, and to the Holy Spirit. As it was in the beginning, is now, and ever shall be, world without end. Amen.

ORATE

My friends, pray that my sacrifice and yours may be acceptable to God the Father almighty.
R. May the Lord receive the sacrifice at your hands, to the praise and glory of his name, for our good and the good of all his holy Church.

PRAYER OVER THE OFFERINGS

Almighty God, may this spiritual oblation which we make to you in memory of the passion, resurrection and ascension of our Lord Jesus Christ, in union with which we offer and present to your divine majesty ourselves, as a holy and living sacrifice, be a praise worthy of your majesty and a means of redemption for us. Through Christ our Lord.
R.Amen.

RITE 3

4 - MERCY

SURSUM CORDA

The Lord be with you.
R. And with your spirit.

Lift up your hearts.
R. We lift them to the Lord.

Let us give thanks to the Lord our God.
R. It is right to give him thanks and praise.

PREFACE

(Further Prefaces are given on pages 108-119)

It is truly worthy and just, right and wholesome, to give you thanks and praise, O holy and eternal God: for in Jesus Christ you call us to glory and virtue, and bestow upon us all things that lead to fullness of life and sanctification. Therefore, we praise you, joining our voices with the celestial choirs and with all the faithful of every time and place who forever sing to the glory of your name:

SANCTUS AND BENEDICTUS

Holy, Holy, Holy, Lord God of Hosts, heaven and earth are full of your glory.
Hosanna in the highest!
Blessed is he + who comes in the name of the Lord.
Hosanna in the highest!

COME AND WORSHIP

EUCHARISTIC PRAYER

Most loving Father, we your servants pray you, through Jesus Christ your Son our Lord, to receive and bless these + gifts, these + oblations, these + holy and immaculate sacrificial offerings.

We offer them for your holy catholic Church, praying that you will be pleased to keep her in peace and unity, to watch over her, and to guide her.

We offer them for our Bishop ......, for all our clergy and faithful, and for all true believers and professors of the catholic and apostolic faith.

We offer them for your entire people: those here present, and all who love and serve you throughout the world (especially ......).

And we offer them for all your children who have gone before us from this world, signed with the seal of faith (especially ......). We pray you, Lord, to lead these, and all who rest in Christ, into the place of refreshment, light and peace.

United in one sacred fellowship we reverently call to mind, first, the holy Lady Mary, mother of our God and Lord Jesus Christ, and then your blessed apostles and martyrs Peter and Paul, and all your glorious saints, who have been the chosen vessels of your grace and lights of the world in their several generations; and we pray that rejoicing in their company and following their good examples, we may be made partakers with them of your heavenly kingdom.

RITE 3

This, then, O Lord, is the offering that we, the servants of your altar, together with your whole household, make to you. Be pleased, O God, wholly to + bless, + approve, and + ratify it, to perfect it and make it worthy of your acceptance, that thus it may become for us the + body and + blood of your dearly beloved Son, our Lord Jesus Christ.

On the day before he suffered, he took bread into his holy and worshipful hands, and with eyes lifted heavenwards to you, God, his almighty Father, and giving thanks to you, he + blessed it, broke it, and gave it to his disciples, saying: Take this, all of you, and eat of it:

FOR THIS IS MY BODY.

In the same way, after supper, taking also this noble chalice into his holy and worshipful hands, again giving you thanks, he + blessed it, and gave it to his disciples, saying: Take this, all of you, and drink of it:

FOR THIS IS MY BLOOD
OF THE NEW AND EVERLASTING COVENANT
– THE MYSTERY OF FAITH –
WHICH IS SHED FOR YOU AND FOR MANY
FOR THE FORGIVENESS OF SINS.

As often as you do these things, you shall do them in memory of me.

Wherefore, O Lord and heavenly Father, we, your humble servants, and with us all your holy people, bearing in mind the ineffable sacrifice of your

COME AND WORSHIP

Son, the mystery of his wondrous incarnation, his blessed passion and precious death, his mighty resurrection and glorious ascension, offer to your sovereign majesty, out of the gifts you have bestowed upon us, this + pure host, + this holy host, + this immaculate host: the + holy bread of life everlasting and the + chalice of eternal salvation.

Deign to regard them with a favourable and gracious countenance, and to accept them as it pleased you to accept the offerings of your servant holy Abel, the sacrifice of our father Abraham, and that of your high priest Melkisedek: a holy sacrifice, an unblemished victim. And we pray you, almighty God, that you would command your holy angel to bear these things to your altar on high, in the sight of your divine majesty, so that those of us who shall have received your Son's most sacred + body and + blood by partaking of the altar here, may be filled with + all grace and heavenly benediction.

It is through Christ that you unceasingly create all these good things, that you + sanctify them, + give them life, + bless them, and bestow them on us.

Through + him, and with + him, and in + him,
are given to you, + God the almighty Father,
in the unity of the + Holy Spirit,
all honour and glory throughout all ages.

R. Amen.

RITE 3

5 - GLORY

THE LORD'S PRAYER

Let us pray. In obedience to the command of our blessed Lord, and following the universal practice of his holy Church, let us say:

Our Father who art in heaven, hallowed be thy name; thy kingdom come, thy will be done on earth as it is in heaven. Give us this day our daily bread; and forgive us our trespasses, as we forgive those who trespass against us. And lead us not into temptation, but deliver us from evil. Amen.

THE FRACTION

Deliver us, O Lord, from all ills, past, present and to come; and of your great and loving kindness, grant peace in our time: that by your aid we may be always free from sin and safe from all adversity.
R. Amen.

The priest breaks the host in half over the paten, places the right hand portion on the paten, breaks a small piece from the left hand portion and places the left hand portion on the paten. Holding the knop of the chalice with the left hand, the priest signs the chalice thrice with the fragment, saying:

The peace + of the Lord + be with you + always.
R. And with your spirit.

COME AND WORSHIP

The priest drops the fragment from the left-hand portion into the chalice, saying:

May this commixture and consecration of the body and blood of our Lord Jesus Christ be for us who receive it a source of everlasting life. Amen.

The priest elevates paten and chalice, saying:

Holy things for the holy!

And all present proclaim:

Jesus Christ is holy.
Jesus Christ is Lord.
To the glory of God the Father.

PRAYER BEFORE COMMUNION

O Son of God, in this sacred banquet in which the memorial of your love is renewed and the pledge of future glory given, grant us so to receive your body and blood that we may be united with you in mystic communion, that we may abide in you and you in us; that we may be renewed in the life of grace; and that our unity with all your church may be deepened and strengthened.
R. Amen.

COMMUNION

The priest receives the body of Christ:

May the body of our Lord Jesus Christ preserve my soul in everlasting life. Amen. +

RITE 3

The priest receives the blood of Christ:

May the blood of our Lord Jesus Christ preserve my soul in everlasting life. Amen.+

The priest administers to clergy and servers, and then to the people.

May the body of our Lord Jesus Christ preserve your soul in everlasting life.
R. Amen.

May the blood of our Lord Jesus Christ preserve your soul in everlasting life.
R. Amen.

THE ABLUTIONS

The sacred vessels are purified. The paten is purified above the chalice. Wine is poured into the chalice over the priest's fingers; then wine and water are together poured into the chalice over the priest's fingers; and finally water is poured into the chalice over the priest's fingers. The sacred vessels are covered.

COMMUNION ADORATION

The following verses of praise, or others, are now said or sung. These may, if desired, be begun during the Ablutions. Or silence may be observed or music played during the Ablutions, preceding the Communion Adoration.

Amen. Praise and glory and wisdom and thanks and honour and power and strength be to our God for ever and ever. Amen.

COME AND WORSHIP

R. To him who sits on the throne and to the Lamb be praise and honour and glory and power, for ever and ever.

POSTCOMMUNION PRAYER

The Lord be with you.
R. And with your spirit.

Let us pray.

The following, or another prayer, is now said.

Almighty God, may we, who in these holy mysteries have been refreshed with your heavenly gifts, be restored in newness of life; and may we glorify your name, not only with our lips but in our lives: by giving ourselves to your service, and by walking in your light all our days; through Christ our Lord.
R. Amen.

RESPONSORY

May the almighty Lord order our days and our times in his peace.
R. May the Lord grant us his peace and eternal life.

GREETING

The Lord be with you.
R. And with your spirit.

RITE 3

DISMISSAL

(1)

The Rite is ended. Go forth in the Light of Christ.
R. Thanks be to God.

(2)

When a procession follows Mass, the conclusion is:

Let us bless the Lord.
R. Thanks be to God.

(3)

For Requiem Mass, the conclusion is:

May the souls of the faithful departed, through
the mercy of God, rest in peace.
R. Amen.

BLESSING

*The priest kisses the altar; then extends, raises and
joins hands, bringing them to repose upon the chest.
The priest says 'May almighty God bless you', and then
gives the blessing with the right hand, the left hand
remaining upon the chest, while saying, 'the Father,
the Son, and the Holy Spirit.'*

May almighty God bless you: the Father, the +
Son, and the Holy Spirit.
R. Amen.

COME AND WORSHIP

INTROIT TEXTS

1

First Sunday of Advent

People of Sion, behold, the Lord comes, and he will save the nations.
You shall have a song, as in the night when a holy solemnity is celebrated, and you shall have gladness of heart, as when one goes with a flute to the mountain of the Lord, to the mighty One of Israel.
Glory be to the Father and to the Son and to the Holy Spirit. As it was in the beginning, is now, and ever shall be, world without end. Amen.
People of Sion, behold, the Lord comes, and he will save the nations.

2

Second Sunday of Advent

O worship the Lord in the beauty of holiness, reverence him all the earth.
Let the heavens rejoice, and let the earth be glad; let the sea roar, and the fullness thereof. Let the field be joyful, and all that is therein: then shall all the trees of the wood rejoice before the Lord, for he comes, he comes to judge the earth.
Glory be to the Father and to the Son and to the Holy Spirit. As it was in the beginning, is now, and ever shall be, world without end. Amen.
O worship the Lord in the beauty of holiness, reverence him all the earth.

INTROIT

3

Third Sunday of Advent

Rejoice in the Lord always; again, I say, Rejoice. Let all people feel the concord that is within you: for the Lord is near.
You have sanctified your world, O Lord, you have averted the captivity of Jacob.
Glory be to the Father and to the Son and to the Holy Spirit. As it was in the beginning, is now, and ever shall be, world without end. Amen.
Rejoice in the Lord always; again, I say, Rejoice. Let all people feel the concord that is within you: for the Lord is near.

4

Fourth Sunday of Advent

Drop down, you heavens, from above, and let the clouds pour forth righteousness. Let the earth be opened, and let her bring forth salvation.
The heavens declare the glory of God, and the firmament proclaims the work of God's hands.
Glory be to the Father and to the Son and to the Holy Spirit. As it was in the beginning, is now, and ever shall be, world without end. Amen.
Drop down, you heavens, from above, and let the clouds pour forth righteousness. Let the earth be opened, and let her bring forth salvation.

COME AND WORSHIP

5

Nativity

Unto us a child is born, unto us a son is given. The sceptre of his power rests upon his shoulder, and his name shall be Angel of Great Counsel.
O sing to the Lord a new song, for the Lord has done wonderful things.
Glory be to the Father and to the Son and to the Holy Spirit. As it was in the beginning, is now, and ever shall be, world without end. Amen.
Unto us a child is born, unto us a son is given. The sceptre of his power rests upon his shoulder, and his name shall be Angel of Great Counsel.

6

Epiphany

Behold, he comes, the Lord, the mighty One; and the kingdom shall be in his hands, and power and dominion.
Give to the king your judgments, O God, and your justice to the king's son.
Glory be to the Father, and to the Son, and to the Holy Spirit. As it was in the beginning, is now, and ever shall be, world without end. Amen.
Behold, he comes, the Lord, the mighty One; and the kingdom shall be in his hands, and power and dominion.

INTROIT

7

Ordinary Time after Epiphany
Also for general use

Righteousness and justice are the foundation of your throne; loving-kindness and faithfulness go before you.
Blessed are those in whose heart is your praise, O Lord, who walk in the light of your presence.
I will sing of the Lord's love for ever; his faithfulness I will proclaim throughout all generations.
Glory be to the Father, and to the Son, and to the Holy Spirit. As it was in the beginning, is now, and ever shall be, world without end. Amen.
Righteousness and justice are the foundation of your throne; loving-kindness and faithfulness go before you.

8

Lent

In every age, Lord, you have been our refuge. From all eternity and for ever you are God. Before the mountains were born, or this earth and our whole world were fashioned, from all eternity and for ever you are God.
Glory be to the Father, and to the Son, and to the Holy Spirit. As it was in the beginning, is now, and ever shall be, world without end. Amen.
In every age, Lord, you have been our refuge.

COME AND WORSHIP

9

Lent

As for me, I will behold your face in righteousness:
I will be satisfied when your glory is manifested.
Hear, O Lord, the voice of my righteousness, and
hearken to my prayer.
Glory be to the Father, and to the Son, and to the
Holy Spirit. As it was in the beginning, is now, and
ever shall be, world without end. Amen.
As for me, I will behold your face in righteousness:
I will be satisfied when your glory is manifested.

10

Lent

To you, I cry, O God: for you will hear me. Incline
your ear to me and hear my words. Show your
wondrous loving kindness, O you who save by your
right hand those who put their trust in you. Keep
me as the apple of your eye, hide me beneath the
shadow of your wings.
Hear, O Lord, the voice of my righteousness, and
hearken to my prayer.
Glory be to the Father, and to the Son, and to the
Holy Spirit. As it was in the beginning, is now, and
ever shall be, world without end. Amen.
To you, I cry, O God: for you will hear me. Incline
your ear to me and hear my words. Show your
wondrous loving kindness, O you who save by your
right hand those who put their trust in you. Keep
me as the apple of your eye, hide me beneath the
shadow of your wings.

INTROIT

11

Lent

Let every heart that seeks the Lord be filled with joy; seek for the Lord, and be strengthened; seek for ever the sacred face.
Praise the Lord, and call upon the holy name: proclaim the works of the Lord to the nations.
Glory be to the Father, and to the Son, and to the Holy Spirit. As it was in the beginning, is now, and ever shall be, world without end. Amen.
Let every heart that seeks the Lord be filled with joy; seek for the Lord, and be strengthened; seek for ever the sacred face.

12

The Cross, the Passion, the Precious Blood

We should glory in the cross of our Lord Jesus Christ, for in him is our hope, our life and our resurrection; through him we are saved and made free.
May God pour forth his love upon us and bless us; may his face shine upon us and may his love enfold us.
Glory be to the Father, and to the Son, and to the Holy Spirit. As it was in the beginning, is now, and ever shall be, world without end. Amen.
We should glory in the cross of our Lord Jesus Christ, for in him is our hope, our life and our resurrection; through him we are saved and made free.

COME AND WORSHIP

13

The Resurrection

I have risen, and I am with you once more!
Alleluia! Alleluia!
O Lord, you have searched me and known me. You
know my resting and my uprising, you understand
my thought from afar.
Glory be to the Father, and to the Son, and to the
Holy Spirit. As it was in the beginning, is now, and
ever shall be, world without end. Amen.
I have risen, and I am with you once more!
Alleluia! Alleluia!

14

Christ in Triumph
Also for general use

At the name of Jesus, every knee shall bow,
whether in heaven, on earth, or in regions far
from the light; and every tongue shall confess that
Jesus Christ is Lord, in the glory of God the
Father.
O Lord, our Lord, how wonderful is your name in
all the earth.
Glory be to the Father, and to the Son, and to the
Holy Spirit. As it was in the beginning, is now, and
ever shall be, world without end. Amen.
At the name of Jesus, every knee shall bow,
whether in heaven, on earth, or in regions far
from the light; and every tongue shall confess that
Jesus Christ is Lord, in the glory of God the
Father.

INTROIT

15

Pentecost

The Spirit of the Lord fills the world, and that which contains all things has knowledge of the voice. Alleluia.
Come, Holy Spirit, fill the hearts of your faithful, and kindle in them the fire of your love.
Glory be to the Father, and to the Son, and to the Holy Spirit. As it was in the beginning, is now, and ever shall be, world without end. Amen.
The Spirit of the Lord fills the world, and that which contains all things has knowledge of the voice. Alleluia.

16

Feast of the Holy Trinity
Also for General Use

Blessed be the Holy Trinity, the undivided Unity.
We will praise God for the loving-kindness that is shown to us. O Lord, our Lord, how wonderful is your name in all the earth.
Glory be to the Father and to the Son and to the Holy Spirit. As it was in the beginning, is now, and ever shall be, world without end. Amen.
Blessed be the Holy Trinity, the undivided Unity.

COME AND WORSHIP

17

Ordinary Time after Trinity

I was glad when they said unto me, Let us go into the house of the Lord. Our feet shall stand within your gates, O Jerusalem.

We have thought of your loving kindness, O God, in the midst of your temple. According to your name, O God, so is your praise to the ends of the earth.

Glory be to the Father and to the Son and to the Holy Spirit. As it was in the beginning, is now, and ever shall be, world without end. Amen.

I was glad when they said unto me, Let us go into the house of the Lord. Our feet shall stand within your gates, O Jerusalem.

18

Feasts of Saints

How lovely is your dwelling-place, O Lord of Hosts. My soul yearns, it faints, for the courts of the Lord; my heart and my flesh cry aloud for the living God.

Better is one day in your courts than a thousand elsewhere. I would rather be a doorkeeper in God's house than dwell in the tents of wickedness.

Glory be to the Father, and to the Son, and to the Holy Spirit. As it was in the beginning, is now, and ever shall be, world without end. Amen.

How lovely is your dwelling-place, O Lord of Hosts. My soul yearns, it faints, for the courts of the Lord; my heart and my flesh cry aloud for the living God.

INTROIT

19

Themes of Redemption

How great is the love that the Father has bestowed on us, that we should be called children of God.
Give thanks to the Lord, and call upon his name; make his deeds known to all the world. Sing to him, praise him, proclaim all his wonderful acts.
Glory be to the Father, and to the Son, and to the Holy Spirit. As it was in the beginning, is now, and ever shall be, world without end. Amen.
How great is the love that the Father has bestowed on us, that we should be called children of God.

20

Feasts of Blessed Mary

A great sign appeared in heaven: a woman, robed in the sun and with the moon beneath her feet, and upon her head a crown of twelve stars.
O sing to the Lord a new song, for the wonderful things he has done.
Glory be to the Father, and to the Son, and to the Holy Spirit. As it was in the beginning, is now, and ever shall be, world without end. Amen.
A great sign appeared in heaven: a woman, robed in the sun and with the moon beneath her feet, and upon her head a crown of twelve stars.

COME AND WORSHIP

21

For General Use

Gathered together, O God, in the midst of your temple, we acknowledge your loving-kindness. Your praise, like your name, reaches to the ends of the earth. Your right hand is filled with justice.
Great is the Lord, and greatly to be praised: in the city of our God, in his holy mountain.
Glory be to the Father, and to the Son, and to the Holy Spirit. As it was in the beginning, is now, and ever shall be, world without end. Amen.
Gathered together, O God, in the midst of your temple, we acknowledge your loving-kindness. Your praise, like your name, reaches to the ends of the earth. Your right hand is filled with justice.

22

For General Use

Not unto us, O Lord, not unto us, but unto your name be the glory, for your love, and for your truth's sake.
Your name endures for all time, O Lord, through all generations you are renowned.
Glory be to the Father, and to the Son, and to the Holy Spirit. As it was in the beginning, is now, and ever shall be, world without end. Amen.
Not unto us, O Lord, not unto us, but unto your name be the glory, for your love, and for your truth's sake.

INTROIT

23

For General Use

O sing unto the Lord a new song, for he has done wonderful things: the right hand and the holy arm of the Lord have gained the victory. The Lord has made salvation known, and righteousness, before the face of all peoples.
Make a joyful noise to the Lord, all the earth: make a mighty noise, and rejoice, and sing praise.
Glory be to the Father, and to the Son, and to the Holy Spirit. As it was in the beginning, is now, and ever shall be, world without end. Amen.
O sing unto the Lord a new song, for he has done wonderful things: the right hand and the holy arm of the Lord have gained the victory. The Lord has made salvation known, and righteousness, before the face of all peoples.

24

For General Use

This is the day that the Lord has made: let us rejoice and be glad in it.
Proclaim it now, O redeemed of the Lord: you whom the Lord has gathered from the corners of the earth.
Glory be to the Father, and to the Son, and to the Holy Spirit. As it was in the beginning, is now, and ever shall be, world without end. Amen.
This is the day that the Lord has made: let us rejoice and be glad in it.

COME AND WORSHIP

25

For General Use

The Lord reigns, let the peoples be in awe; the Lord is enthroned upon the Cherubim, let the earth be moved. The Lord is great in Zion: the Lord is exalted above all. Praise the great and awesome name of the Lord, for it is holy.
Exalt the Lord our God: worship at God's holy mountain: for the Lord our God is holy.
Glory be to the Father, and to the Son, and to the Holy Spirit. As it was in the beginning, is now, and ever shall be, world without end. Amen.
The Lord reigns, let the peoples be in awe; the Lord is enthroned upon the Cherubim, let the earth be moved. The Lord is great in Zion: the Lord is exalted above all. Praise the great and awesome name of the Lord, for it is holy.

26

Requiem

Rest eternal grant unto them, O Lord, and let light perpetual shine upon them.
To you, O God, a hymn of praise is due in Sion, and unto you will the vow be performed in Jerusalem. O you that hear my prayer, unto you shall all flesh come.
Glory be to the Father, and to the Son, and to the Holy Spirit. As it was in the beginning, is now, and ever shall be, world without end. Amen.
Rest eternal grant unto them, O Lord, and let light perpetual shine upon them.

ACCLAMATIONS

GOSPEL ACCLAMATIONS

As appropriate, these texts may be begun and ended with triple alleluias.

1

With all my heart I put my trust in God,
and in him is my strength renewed.

2

O God, you are my God; early will I seek you, my soul thirsts for you.
Your loving-kindness is better than life, my lips shall praise you.
Thus will I bless you while I live, I will lift up my hands in your name.
You have been my help, therefore in the shadow of your wings will I rejoice.

3

Yours, O Lord, is the greatness and the power, and the glory, and the victory, and the majesty. For all that is in the heaven and in the earth is yours. Yours is the kingdom, O Lord, and you are exalted as head over all.

4

Let all those that seek you rejoice and be glad in you. Let such as love your salvation say continually, Let the Lord be magnified.

COME AND WORSHIP

5

God is light, and in him is no darkness at all.
Come, let us walk in the light of the Lord.

6

You are a refuge for the oppressed, a refuge in times of trouble, and those who know your name will put their trust in you.

7

Those who wait upon the Lord shall renew their strength; they shall mount up with wings as eagles; they shall run and not be weary, they shall walk and not be faint.

8

Great and marvelous are your deeds, Lord God almighty. Just and true are your ways, King of the ages. Who will not reverence you, O Lord, and glorify your name? For you alone are holy. All nations will come and worship before you, for your righteous acts have been revealed.

9

Blessed is the people that know the joyful sound: they shall walk, O Lord, in the light of your countenance. In your name shall they rejoice all the day; and in your righteousness shall they be exalted. For you are the glory of their strength; and in your favour shall they rejoice.

ACCLAMATIONS

10

Is it such a fast that I have chosen: a day to afflict
your soul? A day to bow your head as a bulrush,
and to spread sackcloth and ashes under you?
Is not this the fast that I have chosen: to loose the
bands of wickedness, to undo the heavy burdens,
and to let the oppressed go free, and that you
break every yoke?
Is it not to deal your bread to the hungry, and that
you bring the poor and the outcast to your house?

11

The night is far spent, and the day is at hand: let
us therefore cast off the works of darkness, and
let us put on the armour of light.

12

Arise and be doing, and the Lord be with you.
Be steadfast, unmovable, always abounding in the
work of the Lord, forasmuch as you know that
your labour is not in vain in the Lord.
Only, take heed to yourself, and keep your soul
diligently, lest you forget the things which your
eyes have seen, and lest they depart from your
heart.

13

Lo, the winter is past, the rain is over and gone,
the flowers appear on the earth, the time of the
singing of birds is come, and the voice of the dove
is heard in the land. The fig tree puts forth her
green figs, and the vines with the tender grape

COME AND WORSHIP

breathe forth their fragrance.
As the earth brings forth her bud, and as the garden causes all things that are sown in it to spring forth, so the Lord God will cause righteousness and praise to spring forth before all nations.

14

Your word is truth, O Lord: consecrate us in the truth.

15

I am the Way, the Truth and the Life, says the Lord. No one comes to the Father save through me.

16

I am the Resurrection and the Life, says the Lord; whosoever believes in me will never die.

PREFACES

Advent

It is truly worthy and just, right and wholesome, to give you thanks and praise, O holy God, through Jesus Christ our Lord. For the Light of the world has filled us with joy as we prepare to celebrate his birth, and when he comes he will find us watching in prayer, our hearts filled with wonder and love. Therefore we praise you, joining our voices with angels and archangels and with all the faithful of every time and place, who for ever sing to the glory of your name:

Nativity 1

It is truly worthy and just, right and wholesome, to give you thanks and praise, O holy God, creator and ruler of the universe. You created light in the darkness and you brought forth the life of earth. You formed us in your image and called us to love and honour you. When we were unfaithful and turned from your ways, you did not forsake us. In the greatness of your love you delivered us from captivity, made covenant with us, and sent prophets to call us back to the paths of righteousness. In the fullness of time, you sent your only Son to be our Saviour. In him, your Word, dwelling with you from all eternity, became flesh and dwelt among us, full of grace and truth. Therefore, we praise you, joining our voices with the celestial choirs and with the faithful of every time and place who for ever sing to your glory:

COME AND WORSHIP

Nativity 2

It is truly worthy and just, right and wholesome, to give you thanks and praise, O Lord our God, creator and ruler of the universe. For you gave Jesus Christ your only Son to be born at this time for us. By the operation of the Holy Spirit he was made very man of the substance of the Virgin Mary his mother. Through him a new light illumines the world, and heaven and earth embrace. Therefore we praise you, joining our voices with angels and archangels and with all the faithful of every time and place, who for ever sing to the glory of your name:

Nativity (Traditional)

It is truly worthy and just, right and wholesome, to give you thanks and praise, O holy and eternal God. For the light of your glory has flooded the eyes of our mind anew in the mystery of the Word made flesh. Through him, whom we acknowledge as God made visible, we are caught up into the love of things invisible. Therefore we praise you, joining our voices with angels and archangels, with thrones and dominions, and with all the faithful of every time and place, who for ever sing to the glory of your name:

Epiphany

It is truly worthy and just, right and wholesome, to give you thanks and praise, O holy God, through Jesus Christ our Lord. He is the incarnate Word,

PREFACES

the light of the world, full of grace and truth, and in him you have made known your eternal plan of salvation. He is our hope and our life: and his glory shines among us, transforming us to his immortal likeness. Therefore, we praise you, joining our voices with the celestial choirs and with all the faithful of every time and place who for ever sing to the glory of your name:

Lent 1

It is truly worthy and just, right and wholesome, to give you thanks and praise, O God our creator and redeemer. Each year you give us this season of fasting and reflection when we prepare to celebrate the paschal mystery. As we recall, in heart and mind, the great events that give us new life in Christ, so you bring the image of your Son to perfection within us. Therefore, we praise you, joining our voices with choirs of angels and with the faithful of every time and place, who for ever sing to the glory of your name:

Lent 2

It is truly worthy and just, right and wholesome, to give you thanks and praise, O God our creator and redeemer. In your wisdom, you made all things and sustain them by your power. You formed us in your image to love and honour you, but we strayed from the way of your commandments. In the greatness of your love, you did not reject us, but still claimed us as your own. When we were in the house of bondage in Egypt

COME AND WORSHIP

you freed us, and you brought us through the waters of the sea. In the desert you fed us with heavenly manna, and you satisfied our thirst from the desert springs. On the holy mountain you gave us your law to guide us in your way. You led us across the Jordan and into the land of milk and honey. In times of distress you were with us. You spoke again and again through the prophets, calling us to turn from darkness to light, to follow in love the paths of righteousness. And in the fullness of time you sent your only Son, to open for us the way to eternal life. Therefore, we praise you, joining our voices with choirs of angels and with the faithful of every time and place, who for ever sing to the glory of your name:

Easter 1

It is truly worthy and just, right and wholesome, to give you thanks and praise, O holy Lord, almighty Father, eternal God. But chiefly are we bound to praise you for the glorious resurrection of your Son Jesus Christ our Lord. For he is the very Paschal Lamb, which was offered for us, and has taken away the sin of the world; who by his death has destroyed death, and by his rising to life again has restored to us everlasting life. Therefore we praise you, joining our voices with angels and archangels, with thrones and dominions, and with all the faithful of every time and place, who for ever sing to the glory of your name:

PREFACES

Easter 2

It is truly worthy and just, right and wholesome, to give you thanks and praise, O God, creator and ruler of the universe. At your word the Earth was formed, your hand created us from the dust of the earth, and your Spirit gave us life. You placed us among all your creatures to love and serve you and to be guardians of your work. When we were unfaithful to you, your love remained steadfast. When we were prisoners in Egypt, you broke the bonds of our oppression; you brought us through the sea to freedom, you made covenant to be our God. By a pillar of fire you led us through the desert to a land flowing with milk and honey, and you showed us the way of righteousness. You spoke to us through your prophets, and in your Son, the Word made flesh, you lived among us, manifesting your glory; he died that we might live, and is risen again to new life. And because he lives, we shall live also. Therefore we praise you, joining our voices with angels and archangels and with all the faithful of every time and place, who for ever sing to the glory of your name:

Ascension, and seven days after

It is truly worthy and just, right and wholesome, to give you thanks and praise, almighty Father, eternal God, through your dearly beloved Son Jesus Christ our Lord; who after his resurrection manifestly appeared to all his apostles, and in their sight ascended into heaven to prepare a place for us: that where he is, thither we might also ascend and reign with him in glory.

COME AND WORSHIP

Therefore, we praise you, joining our voices with the celestial choirs and with all the faithful of every time and place who for ever sing to the glory of your name:

Pentecost 1

It is truly worthy and just, right and wholesome, to give you thanks and praise, O holy and gracious God, through Jesus Christ our Lord: according to whose most true promise the Holy Spirit manifested with a sudden great sound, as it had been a mighty wind, in the likeness of fiery tongues, lighting upon the apostles, to teach them, and to lead them to all truth. Therefore, we praise you, joining our voices with choirs of angels, with prophets, apostles and martyrs, and with all the faithful of every time and place, who for ever sing to the glory of your name:

Pentecost 2

It is truly worthy and just, right and wholesome, to give you thanks and praise, eternal God, creator and ruler of the universe. With the right arm of your power, you shaped this world and all that is in it. By your Holy Spirit, you breathed life into our human form, and set us on the earth to praise and honour you. When we strayed from the paths of righteousness, your truth and light inspired your prophets to call us to return to you. In the fullness of time, you sent your Son Jesus Christ to be our redeemer. In every age, O Lord, your strength has been our support, and the light

PREFACES

of your Spirit has guided us upon the path of life. Therefore, we praise you, joining our voices with choirs of angels, with prophets, apostles and martyrs, and with all the faithful of every time and place, who for ever sing to the glory of your name:

Trinity

It is truly worthy and just, right and wholesome, to give you thanks and praise, almighty Father, eternal God; for you have revealed your glory as the glory also of the Son and of the Holy Spirit: three persons equal in majesty, united in essence, undivided in splendour, yet one Lord, one God, ever to be adored in your everlasting glory. Therefore we praise you, joining our voices with angels and archangels, with Cherubim and Seraphim, and with all the faithful of every time and place, who for ever sing to the glory of your name:

Common Preface 1

It is truly worthy and just, right and wholesome, to give you thanks and praise, almighty God, through Christ our Lord. Through him the angels and archangels and all the hosts of heaven adore, praise and revere your majesty. Therefore, we too praise you, joining our voices with the celestial choirs and with all the faithful of every time and place who for ever sing to the glory of your name:

COME AND WORSHIP

Common Preface 2

It is truly worthy and just, right and wholesome, to give you thanks and praise, O holy and eternal God: for in Jesus Christ you call us to glory and virtue, and bestow upon us all things that lead to fullness of life and sanctification. Therefore, we praise you, joining our voices with the celestial choirs and with all the faithful of every time and place who for ever sing to the glory of your name:

Common Preface 3

It is truly worthy and just, right and wholesome, to give you thanks and praise, O holy God, through Christ our Lord: for he is the true High Priest, who has freed us from our failings and has made us to be a kingdom and priests unto you our God and Father. Therefore, we praise you, joining our voices with choirs of angels and with the faithful of every time and place, who for ever sing to the glory of your name:

Common Preface 4

It is truly worthy and just, right and wholesome, to give you thanks and praise, O strong and faithful God. In the beginning your Word summoned light, the night withdrew, and creation dawned. As the aeons unfolded, waters gathered on the face of the earth; then life appeared, and began its journey. When the earth had grown full in the abundance of its diversity, you created us in your image and made us stewards of your

PREFACES

creation: rational creatures, who would grow in knowledge of you and extol the glory and goodness of your works. Therefore, we praise you, joining our voices with choirs of angels and with the faithful of every time and place, who for ever sing to the glory of your name:

Transfiguration

It is truly worthy and just, right and wholesome, to give you thanks and praise, almighty Father, eternal God, through Christ the Lord: because the divine glory of the Incarnate Word shone forth upon the holy mount before the chosen witnesses of his majesty, and your own voice from heaven proclaimed your beloved Son. Therefore we praise you, joining our voices with angels and archangels and with all the faithful of every time and place, who for ever sing to the glory of your name:

Presentation

It is truly worthy and just, right and wholesome, to give you thanks and praise, O holy and gracious God. For your Son, born of the Virgin Mary, was this day presented in the temple and revealed by the Holy Spirit as the light and hope of all nations. Therefore we praise you, joining our voices with angels and archangels and with all the faithful of every time and place, who for ever sing to the glory of your name:

COME AND WORSHIP

Annunciation

It is truly worthy and just, right and wholesome, to give you thanks and praise, O Lord our God. For receiving your word in faith, and in complete accord with your will, the Virgin Mary conceived by the power of the Holy Spirit, and gave birth to your Son. In him, the prince of peace, our redemption is accomplished. Therefore we praise you, joining our voices with angels and archangels and with all the faithful of every time and place, who for ever sing to the glory of your name:

All Saints

It is truly worthy and just, right and wholesome, to give you thanks and praise, O holy Lord, almighty Father, eternal God, through Christ our Lord. In the righteousness of your saints you have shown us the pattern of the spiritual life, and in their blessedness a glorious pledge of the hope of our calling: that, being compassed about with so great a crowd of witnesses, we may run with patience the race that is set before us, and may with them attain the unfading crown of glory. Therefore, we praise you, joining our voices with the celestial choirs and with all the faithful of every time and place who for ever sing to the glory of your name:

Saints' Days

It is truly worthy and just, right and wholesome, to give you thanks and praise, O Lord our God. For

PREFACES

your glory is revealed in (N ......, and in) all the Saints. In their lives we are given a noble example of devotion to Christ, and in their holiness we find inspiration. Therefore, we praise you, joining our voices with the celestial choirs and with all the faithful of every time and place who for ever sing to the glory of your name:

The Virgin Mary

It is truly worthy and just, right and wholesome, to give you thanks and praise, O Lord our God. For you gave Jesus Christ your only Son to be born for our salvation: who by the operation of the Holy Spirit was made very man of the substance of the Virgin Mary, the mystical rose and vessel of holiness whom all generations shall call blessed. Therefore we praise you, joining our voices with choirs of angels, with prophets, apostles and martyrs, and with all the faithful of every time and place, who for ever sing to the glory of your name:

The Holy Cross

It is truly worthy and just, right and wholesome, to give you thanks and praise, O Holy and Immortal God. For you decreed that salvation should come through the wood of the cross, that the tree of defeat should become the tree of victory. Herein shines forth the mystery of the Cross, that where life was lost, there, through Christ our Lord, life should be restored. Therefore, we praise you, joining our voices with

COME AND WORSHIP

the celestial choirs and with all the faithful of every time and place who for ever sing to the glory of your name:

Christ the King

It is truly worthy and just, right and wholesome, to give you thanks and praise, O holy Lord, almighty Father, eternal God: for you anointed your only-begotten Son, our Lord Jesus Christ, with the oil of gladness to be a priest for ever and king of all the universe, so that by giving himself as an unblemished sacrifice and peace-offering on the altar of the cross he might accomplish the mystery of our redemption; and that, all creation being subdued to his rule, he might hand over a universal and everlasting kingdom to your boundless majesty: a kingdom of truth and life, of holiness and grace, of justice, of love and of peace. Therefore we praise you, joining our voices with angels and archangels, with thrones and dominions, and with all the faithful of every time and place, who for ever sing to the glory of your name:

The Departed

It is truly right, our duty and our salvation, to give you thanks and praise, O holy Lord, almighty Father, eternal God, through Christ our Lord. For in him, who rose glorious from the tomb, the way of eternal life is opened for us, and the shadow of death is banished in the splendour of light's triumph. Therefore we praise you, joining our

PREFACES

voices with angels and archangels, with thrones
and dominions, and with all the faithful of every
time and place, who for ever sing to the glory of
your name:

COME AND WORSHIP

OFFERTORY TEXTS

1

I am come that you might have life, and that you might have it more abundantly.

2

Come unto me, all you that labour and are heavy laden, and I will refresh you. Take my yoke upon you, and learn of me, for I am meek and humble in heart, and you shall find rest for your souls; for my yoke is easy and my burden is light.

3

Beloved, let us love one another, for love is of God, and every one that loves is born of God and knows God.

4

God is love; and he that dwells in love, dwells in God. Herein is love, not that we loved God, but that he loved us, and sent his Son to be the propitiation for our sins.

5

As now the supper of the Lord is spread before you, lift up your hearts and minds above all faithless fears and cares, rejoicing in the grace of

OFFERTORY

our Lord Jesus Christ, the love of God, and the fellowship of the Holy Spirit.

6

Hear what comfortable words our Saviour Christ says unto all that truly turn to him.
Come unto me all that travail and are heavy laden, and I will refresh you.
God so loved the world that he gave his only-begotten Son, to the end that all that believe in him should not perish, but have everlasting life.
Hear also what Saint Paul says. This is a true saying, and worthy of all people to be received, that Christ Jesus came into the world to save sinners.
Hear also what Saint John says. If any one sin, we have an Advocate with the Father, Jesus Christ the righteous; and he is the propitiation for our sins.

7

Behold, I stand at the door, and knock: if any hear my voice and open the door, I will come in to them, and sup with them, and they with me.

8

Labour not for the food which perishes, but for that which endures unto everlasting life, which the Son of Man shall give unto you.

COME AND WORSHIP

9

God, who commanded the light to shine out of the darkness, has shined in our hearts, to give the light of the knowledge of the glory of God in the face of Jesus Christ.

10

I am the Light of the world. The one that follows me shall not walk in darkness but shall have the light of life.

11

Melchizedek king of Salem brought forth bread and wine; and he was the priest of the most high God.

12

Lord Jesus Christ, King of Glory, may your holy angel and standard-bearer blessed Michael bring the souls of all the faithful departed into your holy light.

13

You have the words of eternal life, O Lord. To you we give ourselves, and these gifts of bread and wine; for you are worthy, O Lord, to receive glory and honour and power: for you have created all things, and for your pleasure they are and were created.

Offices

COME AND WORSHIP

OFFICE OF PRIME

MORNING PRAYER

THE PSALMS FOR PRIME

SUNDAY, 5, 13, 21; MONDAY, 2, 10, 18; TUESDAY, 6, 14, 22; WEDNESDAY, 3, 11, 19; THURSDAY, 7, 15, 23; FRIDAY, 4, 12, 20; SATURDAY, 8, 16, 24.

INVOCATION

All make the sign of the cross as the priest says:

In the name of the Father, and of + the Son, and of the Holy Spirit.
R. Amen.

PREPARATION

Sing, O heavens, and be joyful, O earth;
R. Break forth into singing, O mountains.

For the Lord God omnipotent reigns.
R. Let us be glad, and rejoice, and give honour to our God.

O magnify the Lord with me, and let us exalt the holy name for ever.
R. Blessed be the name of the Lord, from this time forth and for evermore.

PRIME

Day by day we magnify the Lord.
R. Every day we bless our God.

Let us praise the holy name.
R. From the rising to the setting of the sun, the Lord's holy name be praised.

CONFESSION

Our help is in the name of the Lord.
R. Who made heaven and earth.

After a period of silence for private recollection of failings the following is said by all:

I confess to almighty God, the Father, the Son and the Holy Spirit, that I have sinned in thought, word and deed, through my own most grievous fault. Wherefore I pray almighty God to have mercy upon me, to forgive me all my sins, and to bring me to everlasting life.

ABSOLUTION

If a priest is conducting the Office, the Absolution is now given:

May the almighty and loving Lord, the God of all mercy, grant us + forgiveness and perfect remission of our sins, time for amendment of life, and the grace and comfort of the Holy Spirit.
R. Amen.

COME AND WORSHIP

COLLECT

The Lord be with you.
R. And with your spirit.

Let us pray.

O God, you have folded back the mantle of the night to enrobe us in the golden glory of the day. Banish from our hearts, we pray you, all unworthy thoughts, and make us glad with the brightness of hope; that we may effectively aspire to unwon virtues and new challenges in your Son, our Saviour Jesus Christ. Through the same Lord Jesus Christ, who lives and reigns with you and the Holy Spirit, one God, throughout all ages.
R. Amen.

HYMN

A suitable hymn may be sung.

PSALMODY

The psalms of the day, each being used in whole or in part, are now chanted or said. At the conclusion of each psalm is said:

Glory be to the Father, and to the Son: and to the Holy Spirit.
R. As it was in the beginning, is now, and ever shall be: world without end. Amen.

PRIME

FIRST READING

The Epistle of the day is read, after which is said:

This is the Word of the Lord.
R. Thanks be to God.

TE DEUM LAUDAMUS

We praise you, O God: we acknowledge you to be the Lord.
All the earth worships you: the Father everlasting.
To you all angels cry aloud: the heavens and all the powers therein.
To you Cherubim and Seraphim: continually do cry,
Holy, holy, holy: Lord God of Hosts,
Heaven and earth are filled: with the majesty of your glory.
The glorious company of the apostles: gives you praise.
The goodly company of prophets: gives you praise.
The noble army of martyrs: gives you praise.
Holy Church throughout the world: acknowledges you,
The Father: of an infinite majesty,
Your adorable, true: and only Son,
And the Holy Spirit: the Comforter.
You are the king of glory: O Christ.
You are the everlasting Son: of the Father.

When you took it upon you to deliver us: you did not disdain the Virgin's womb.
When you overcame the sharpness of death: you opened the kingdom of heaven to all believers.
You are seated at the right hand of God: in the glory of the Father.
We believe that you shall come: to be our judge.
We therefore pray you, aid your servants: whom you have redeemed with your precious blood.
Make them to be numbered with your saints: in glory everlasting.

HYMN

A second suitable hymn may be sung.

SECOND READING

The Gospel of the day is read, after which is said:

This is the Word of the Lord.
R. Thanks be to God.

MEDITATION

The Lord is in his holy temple.
R. Let all the earth keep silence before him.

A period of quietness, of reflection, is observed.

PRIME

SHORT CHAPTER

Honour and glory throughout all ages to our king, eternal, immortal, invisible, who alone is God.
R. Thanks be to God.

RESPONSORY

Jesus Christ, Son of the Living God, pour forth your love upon us.
R. Jesus Christ, Son of the Living God, pour forth your love upon us.

You who sit at God's right hand.
R. Pour forth your love upon us.

Glory be to the Father, and to the Son, and to the Holy Spirit.
R. Jesus Christ, Son of the Living God, pour forth your love upon us.

Arise, O Lord, and grant us your aid.
R. Deliver us, O Lord, for your name's sake.

SPIRITUAL AFFIRMATIONS

There is one Body and One Spirit.
One Lord, one Faith, one Baptism.
One God and Parent of us all, who is above all, through all, and in all.

COME AND WORSHIP

COLLECT

The Lord be with you.
R. And with your spirit.

Let us pray.

The president says the Collect of the day, and then one or more of the following Collects:

(1)

From the night our spirit awakens to you, O God, for your precepts are our light. Make known to us, O God, your righteousness, your commandments and your judgments. Enlighten the eyes of our minds. Drive away all darkness from our hearts. Grant us to behold the dawn and the day with joyfulness. By the seal of your Holy Spirit, guard our lives from all reproach, and guide our steps in the way of peace. Through Christ our Lord.
R. Amen.

(2)

O God, author of peace and lover of concord, in the knowledge of whom stands our eternal life, whose service is perfect freedom: defend us, your children, from all assaults of the enemy; so that, trusting in your protection, we may not fear the power of our adversaries. Through Jesus Christ our Lord.
R. Amen.

PRIME

(3)

O Lord our God, shield us by your mighty power during this day, and of your loving-kindness grant that we may not fall into sin, neither enter into any danger; but that all our thoughts, our words and our deeds, may be directed in perfect harmony with your will. Through Christ our Lord.
R. Amen.

THE LORD'S PRAYER

Lord, pour forth your love upon us.
R. Christ, embrace us with your love.
Lord, uplift us in your love.

All now say:

Our Father who art in heaven, hallowed be thy name; thy kingdom come, thy will be done on earth as it is in heaven. Give us this day our daily bread; and forgive us our trespasses, as we forgive those who trespass against us. And lead us not into temptation, but deliver us from evil. Amen.

CONCLUSION

We shall go forward, O Lord, in the light of your countenance.

COME AND WORSHIP

R. In your name we shall rejoice all the day, and in your righteousness we shall be exalted.

For you are the glory of our strength.
R. In your loving regard we are blessed.

The Lord be with you.
R. And with your spirit.

Let us bless the Lord.
R. Thanks be to God.

May the almighty and loving Lord, the Father and the Son and the Holy Spirit, + bless us and keep us, and bring us to everlasting life.
R. Amen.

VESPERS

OFFICE OF VESPERS

EVENING PRAYER

THE PSALMS FOR VESPERS

SUNDAY, 125, 133, 141; MONDAY, 122, 130, 138;
TUESDAY, 126, 134, 142; WEDNESDAY, 123, 131, 139;
THURSDAY, 127, 135, 143; FRIDAY, 124, 132, 140;
SATURDAY, 128, 136, 144.

INVOCATION

All make the sign of the cross as the priest says:

In the name of the Father, and of + the Son, and
of the Holy Spirit.
R. Amen.

PREPARATION

O holy One, God of glory, bestow upon us the
spirit of wisdom and revelation in the knowledge
of your Christ.
**R. Let the eyes of our understanding be
enlightened, O Lord.**

With you, O God, is the fountain of life.
R. In your light shall we see light.

Glory be to the Father, and to the Son, and to the
Holy Spirit.

COME AND WORSHIP

R. As it was in the beginning, is now, and ever shall be, world without end. Amen.

CONFESSION

Our help + is in the name of the Lord.
R. Who made heaven and earth.

After a period of silence for private recollection of failings the following is said by all:

I confess to almighty God, the Father, the Son and the Holy Spirit, that I have sinned in thought, word and deed, through my own most grievous fault. Wherefore I pray almighty God to have mercy upon me, to forgive me all my sins, and to bring me to everlasting life.

ABSOLUTION

If a priest is conducting the Office, the Absolution is now given:

May the almighty and loving Lord, the God of all mercy, grant us + forgiveness and perfect remission of our sins, time for amendment of life, and the grace and comfort of the Holy Spirit.
R. Amen.

VESPERS

COLLECT

The Lord be with you.
R. And with your spirit.

Let us pray.

Almighty God, to whom all hearts are open, all desires known, and from whom no secrets are hidden, cleanse the thoughts of our hearts by the inspiration of your Holy Spirit, that we may perfectly love you, and worthily magnify your holy name; through Christ our Lord.
R. Amen.

PSALMODY

The psalms of the day, each being used in whole or in part, are now chanted or said. At the conclusion of each psalm is said:

Glory be to the Father, and to the Son: and to the Holy Spirit.
R. As it was in the beginning, is now, and ever shall be: world without end. Amen.

SHORT CHAPTER

Blessed be the God and Father of our Lord Jesus Christ, the most loving Father and God of all consolation, who comforts us in every trial.
R. Thanks be to God.

COME AND WORSHIP

HYMN

A suitable hymn may be sung.

INCENSATION

The priest blesses incense:

May you be blessed by the one in whose honour you are to burn. Amen

Standing before the altar, holding the censer, the priest says:

May my prayer rise up to you like fragrant incense, Lord, like an evening offering from my outstretched hands.

The Magnificat is now said or sung, as the priest offers incense to God, censing the altar.

MAGNIFICAT

My soul magnifies the Lord: and my spirit rejoices in God my Saviour.
For he has regarded: the lowliness of his hand-maiden.
For behold, from henceforth: all generations shall call me blessed.
For he that is mighty has magnified me: and holy

VESPERS

is his name.
And his mercy is on those who reverence him:
throughout all generations.
He has shown strength with his arm: he has
scattered the proud in the imagination of their
hearts.
He has put down the mighty from their seat: and
has exalted the humble and meek.
He has filled the hungry with good things: and the
rich he has sent empty away.
He remembering his mercy has helped his servant
Israel: as he promised to our forefathers, Abraham
and his posterity, for ever.
Glory be to the Father, and to the Son: and to the
Holy Spirit.
As it was in the beginning, is now, and ever shall
be: world without end. Amen.

COLLECTS

The Lord be with you.
R. And with your spirit.

Let us pray.

*The Collect of the day is first read, and then the
following two Collects:*

Keep our hearts, O Lord, in that realm of the
Spirit where the mind is without fear and the head
is held high, where knowledge is wide, where

COME AND WORSHIP

words come from the depths of truth; where
tireless striving wins towards perfection; where
the clear stream of reason loses not its way but
flows on in deeper thought and ever widening
action; where faith becomes living certainty;
where noblest aspiration meets with Christ and
finds fulfillment in his Light. Through the same
Christ our Lord.
R. Amen.

Lord of all power and might, author and giver of
all good things: graft in our hearts, we pray you,
the love of your name; increase in us true religion;
nourish us with all goodness; and, of your great
and loving kindness, so guide us through this
earthly pilgrimage that we may be found worthy
of eternal life. Through Jesus Christ our Lord.
R. Amen.

THE LORD'S PRAYER

Lord, pour forth your love upon us.
R. Christ, embrace us with your love.
Lord, uplift us in your love.

All now say:

**Our Father who art in heaven, hallowed be thy
name; thy kingdom come, thy will be done on
earth as it is in heaven. Give us this day our
daily bread; and forgive us our trespasses, as we
forgive those who trespass against us. And lead
us not into temptation, but deliver us from evil.
Amen.**

VESPERS

CONCLUSION

O God, you are my God; early will I seek you.
R. My soul thirsts for you.

Your loving kindness is better than life.
R. My lips shall praise you.

Thus will I bless you while I live.
R. I will lift up my hands in your name.

You have been my help.
R. Therefore in the shadow of your wings I will rejoice.

The Lord be with you.
R. And with your spirit.

Let us bless the Lord.
R. Thanks be to God.

May the almighty and loving Lord, the Father and the Son and the Holy Spirit, + bless us and keep us, and bring us to everlasting life.
R. Amen.

COME AND WORSHIP

OFFICE OF COMPLINE

NIGHT PRAYER

THE PSALMS FOR COMPLINE

SUNDAY, 29, 37, 45; MONDAY, 26, 34, 42; TUESDAY, 30, 38, 46; WEDNESDAY, 27, 35, 43; THURSDAY, 31, 39, 47; FRIDAY, 28, 36, 44; SATURDAY, 32, 40, 48.

This is a reflective, peaceful service. It is a time for 'winding down'. Ideally, it should end the day's activities. The psalms and the Nunc Dimittis may be said or chanted by all together; or they may be said or chanted antiphonally.

INVOCATION

All make the sign of the cross with the priest, as he says:

In the name of the Father, and of the Son, and of the Holy Spirit.
R. Amen.

PREPARATION

May the almighty Lord grant us a quiet night and a perfect end.
R. Amen.

COMPLINE

Christians, be sober, be vigilant. Your adversary the devil, as a roaring lion, walks about, seeking always whom to devour. Be strong in the faith, resist him!

But you, O Lord, pour forth your love upon us.
R. Thanks be to God.

CONFESSION

Our help is in the name of the Lord.
R. Who made heaven and earth.

After a period of silence for private recollection of failings the following is said by all:

I confess to almighty God, the Father, the Son and the Holy Spirit, that I have sinned in thought, word and deed, through my own most grievous fault. Wherefore I pray almighty God to have mercy upon me, to forgive me all my sins, and to bring me to everlasting life.

ABSOLUTION

If a priest is conducting the Office, the Absolution is now given:

May the almighty and loving Lord, the God of all mercy, grant us + forgiveness and perfect

COME AND WORSHIP

remission of our sins, time for amendment of life,
and the grace and comfort of the Holy Spirit.
R. Amen.

COLLECT

Living God, you have built your Church upon the
foundation of the apostles and prophets, Jesus
Christ himself being the head corner stone: grant
us, we pray you, so to be joined together in unity
of spirit by their proclamation of your truth, that
we may be made a holy temple acceptable to you.
Through the same Christ our Lord.
R. Amen.

PSALMODY

*The psalms of the day, each being used in whole or in
part, are now chanted or said. At the conclusion of
each psalm is said:*

Glory be to the Father, and to the Son: and to the
Holy Spirit.
**R. As it was in the beginning, is now, and ever
shall be: world without end. Amen.**

HYMN

A suitable hymn may be sung.

COMPLINE

READING

One of the following, or another appropriate text, is now read.

(1)

Jeremiah 14: 9

Your dwelling place is among us, O Lord, and your holy name is invoked upon us. Let us never be parted from you, O Lord, our God.

(2)

1 John 4: 7-12

Beloved, let us love one another, for love is of God. Every person that loves is born of God, and knows God.
The one that loves not, that one does not know God; for God is love.
In this was God's love manifested towards us: that he sent his Son into the world that we might live through him.
Herein is love, not that we loved God, but that he loved us, and sent his Son to be the propitiation for our sins.
Beloved, if God so loved us, we ought also to love one another.
No one has seen God at any time; but if we love one another God dwells in us, and his love is perfected in us.

COME AND WORSHIP

MEDITATION

The Lord is in his holy temple.
R. Let all the earth keep silence before him.

A period of quietness, a time for reflection, is observed.

RESPONSORY

Into your hands, O Lord, I commend my spirit.
R. Into your hands, O Lord, I commend my spirit.

For you have redeemed me, O Lord, God of truth.
R. Into your hands, O Lord, I commend my spirit.

Glory be to the Father, and to the Son, and to the Holy Spirit.
R. Into your hands, O Lord, I commend my spirit.

Guard us, Lord, as the apple of your eye.
R. Protect us beneath the shadow of your wings.

NUNC DIMITTIS

ANTHEM
Shield us, Lord, in our waking hours, and watch

COMPLINE

over us while we sleep: that awake we may watch with Christ, and asleep we may rest in peace.

NUNC DIMITTIS

Lord, now let your servant depart in peace: according to your word;
for my eyes have seen your salvation: which you have prepared before the face of all people; to be a light to lighten the Gentiles: and to be the glory of your people Israel.
Glory be to the Father and to the Son: and to the Holy Spirit.
As it was in the beginning, is now, and ever shall be: world without end. Amen.

ANTHEM

Shield us, Lord, in our waking hours, and watch over us while sleeping: that awake we may watch with Christ, and asleep we may rest in peace.

COLLECTS

The Lord be with you.
R. And with your spirit.

Let us pray.

The Collect of the day is said, and then one or more of the following Collects:

COME AND WORSHIP

(1)

Visit this place, O Lord, and drive far from it all the snares of the enemy. Let your holy angels be with us to keep us in peace, and may your blessing rest upon us always. Through Jesus Christ our Lord.
R. Amen.

(2)

Lighten our darkness, we pray you, Lord, and in your great and loving kindness defend us from all harm during this night, for the love of your only Son, our Saviour Jesus Christ.
R. Amen.

(3)

Be present, O most loving God, and protect us through the silence and darkness of this night, so that we who are wearied by the changes and chances of this fleeting world, may repose upon your eternal changelessness. Through Jesus Christ our Lord.
R. Amen.

(4)

Look down, O Lord, from your heavenly throne, illuminate this night with your celestial

COMPLINE

brightness, and from the children of light banish
the deeds of darkness. Through Jesus Christ our
Lord.
R. Amen.

THE LORD'S PRAYER

Lord, pour forth your love upon us.
R. Christ, embrace us with your love.
Lord, uplift us in your love.

All now say:

**Our Father who art in heaven, hallowed be thy
name; thy kingdom come, thy will be done on
earth as it is in heaven. Give us this day our
daily bread; and forgive us our trespasses, as we
forgive those who trespass against us. And lead
us not into temptation, but deliver us from evil.
Amen.**

CONCLUSION

I will lay me down in peace, and take my rest.
**R. For you alone, Lord, make me dwell in
safety.**

The Lord be with you.
R. And with your spirit.

COME AND WORSHIP

Let us bless the Lord.
R. Thanks be to God.

May the almighty and loving Lord, the Father and the Son and the Holy Spirit, + bless us and watch over us.
R. Amen.

ASPERSION

If a priest is conducting the Office, the participants may here, in silence, be sprinkled with holy water.

Rite of Baptism
Visitation
Confession
Funeral Rites

COME AND WORSHIP

RITE OF BAPTISM

If a deacon conducts the Rite of Baptism, the salt and water that he uses shall have been previously blessed by a priest. When an infant is to be baptised the responses are made by the sponsor, but candidates who are of viable age, able to speak and to understand, make the responses for themselves.

1 - THE INSPIRING BREATH

PRELIMINARY CHARGE

The priest, wearing a violet stole, greets the candidate and sponsors at the entrance to the church, or in the narthex. The priest asks the name of the candidate, and then says:

What do you ask of the Church of God?
R. The Faith.

What does the Faith promise you?
R. Eternal life.

If you have life, keep the commandments: You shall love the Lord your God with your whole heart, your whole soul and your whole mind; and your neighbour as yourself.

BAPTISM

EXSUFFLATION AND FIRST EXORCISM

The priest then breathes gently upon the candidate's face or head thrice, in the form of a cross.

May all unworthiness depart from you, that you may be a pure vessel for the Holy Spirit.

THE FIRST SIGNING WITH THE CROSS

Using the thumb, the priest signs the cross on the candidate's forehead and breast, saying:

Receive the sign of the cross upon + your brow and upon + your heart. Henceforth, let your life be so governed by celestial precepts that you may be a living and worthy temple of God.

Let us pray.

In your great and loving kindness, O Lord, be pleased to hear our prayers, and with your never-failing power protect N, your elect, signed now with the sign of Christ's cross. May this elect, continually regarding this experience of your great glory and keeping your commandments, attain the glory of regeneration. Through Christ our Lord. **R. Amen.**

COME AND WORSHIP

2 - THE RECEIVING BODY

LAYING-ON OF HANDS

The priest imposes the right hand on the candidate's head, and then with the right hand still outstretched says:

Let us pray.

Almighty and everlasting God, Father of our Lord Jesus Christ, graciously regard *N*, your servant, whom you have brought to the Faith. Let all blindness of heart be driven from him (her), let all unworthy bonds be broken, and let the door of your great and loving kindness be opened to him (her). Established in the symbol of your wisdom, may he (she) be free from all ills, and may he (she) spread about him (her) the fragrance of your precepts, joyfully serving you in your Church and growing daily in holiness. Through Christ our Lord.
R. Amen.

THE GIVING OF SALT

The priest places a small amount of blessed salt in the candidate's mouth.

N, receive the salt of wisdom; may it advance you in the attainment of eternal life.
R. Amen.

Peace be with you.
R. And with your spirit.

BAPTISM

Let us pray.

O God of our ancestors, O God in whom is the beginning of all truth: in your love, look upon *N,* your servant, now tasting blessed salt. Let him (her) hunger no more, but fill him (her) with celestial food, that he (she) may always be joyful in spirit and fervent in hope, in the service of your name. Lead him (her), we pray you, to the waters of the new regeneration, that with all your faithful he (she) may merit the eternal reward of your promises. Through Christ our Lord.
R. Amen.

SECOND EXORCISM

The priest makes the sign of the cross thrice over the candidate, as indicated, saying:

Let all influences of darkness and deceits of the enemy depart from *N,* in the name of + the Father, and of + the Son, and of + the Holy Spirit; for by the living and true God, and our Lord Jesus Christ, this elect has been called to holy grace, to blessing, and to the baptismal font.

SECOND SIGNING WITH THE CROSS

The priest makes the sign of the cross on the candidate's brow:

And let this sign of + the holy cross, which we place upon his (her) brow, never be violated by the powers of darkness. Through Christ our Lord.
R. Amen.

COME AND WORSHIP

SECOND LAYING-ON OF HANDS

Let us pray.

Holy Lord, omnipotent and eternal God, author of light and of truth: let your never-failing, most just, loving-kindness rest upon this elect. Enlighten him (her) with the light of your own understanding, purify him (her) and sanctify him (her), and grant him (her) true knowledge: that being thus fitted for the grace of your baptism, he (she) may abound in firm hope, in right counsel, and in holy doctrine. Through Christ our Lord. **R. Amen.**

BAPTISM

3 - JUSTICE

CREED AND LORD'S PRAYER

The priest places the end of the stole upon the candidate, saying:

N, enter the temple of God, that you may have part with Christ in life eternal.

With the end of the stole remaining upon the candidate, the priest leads the candidate and the sponsors into the body of the church. As they process, the Apostles' Creed and the Lord's Prayer are said by priest and sponsors, or by priest and candidate:

I believe in God the Father almighty, creator of heaven and earth, and in Jesus Christ his only Son our Lord, who was conceived by the Holy Spirit, born of the virgin Mary, suffered under Pontius Pilate, was crucified, died and was buried. He descended into hell; on the third day he rose again from the dead and ascended into heaven; he is seated at the right hand of God the Father almighty, and he shall come again to judge both the living and the dead. I believe in the Holy Spirit, the holy catholic Church, the communion of saints, the forgiveness of sins, the resurrection of the body, and the life everlasting. Amen.

The end of the priest's stole is removed from the candidate, and the Lord's Prayer is said:

Our Father who art in heaven, hallowed be thy name; thy kingdom come, thy will be done on

COME AND WORSHIP

earth as it is in heaven. Give us this day our daily bread; and forgive us our trespasses, as we forgive those who trespass against us. And lead us not into temptation, but deliver us from evil. Amen.

FINAL EXORCISM

The priest addresses the candidate, signing the cross as indicated:

N, servant of God, let every force of darkness, let all unworthiness and hindrance, depart from you: in the name of + the Father almighty, in the name of + Jesus Christ, his Son, our Lord and Judge, and in the power of + the Holy Spirit. For the Lord has called you into his holy temple, that you yourself may be made a temple of the living God, and that the Holy Spirit may dwell within you. Through Christ our Lord.
R. Amen.

EPHPHETA

The priest, using both hands, touches the candidate's ears, saying once:

Ephpheta, be open!

With one hand, the priest lightly touches the candidate nostrils, saying:

To the fragrance of sweetness!

The priest concludes the 'opening':

BAPTISM

But you, O powers of darkness, be far from here, for the judgment of God is at hand!

THE THREE RENUNCIATIONS

The priest addresses the candidate:

Do you renounce Satan?
R. I do renounce him.

And all his works?
R. I do renounce them.

And all his vain glories and deceits?
R. I do renounce them.

ANOINTING WITH OIL OF CATECHUMENS

The priest anoints the candidate on the throat and on the nape of the neck, signing the crosses with Oil of Catechumens.

I anoint you + with this saving Oil, in + Christ Jesus our Lord, that you may have eternal life.

COME AND WORSHIP

4 - MERCY

THE THREE AFFIRMATIONS

The priest assumes a white stole and proceeds to the font, followed by sponsors and candidate. The priest addresses the candidate:

Do you believe in God the Father almighty, creator of heaven and earth?
R. I do believe.

Do you believe in Jesus Christ, his only Son our Lord, who was incarnate in this world and who suffered for us?
R. I do believe.

Do you believe in the Holy Spirit, the holy catholic Church, the communion of saints, the forgiveness of sins, the resurrection of the body and the life everlasting?
R. I do believe.

At the font the candidate, if an infant, is held by one of the sponsors, while the right hand of the other sponsor rests upon the candidate's shoulder; otherwise, the candidate able to answer for himself or herself stands without the touch of a sponsor.

N, do you desire to be baptised?
R. I do.

MATTER AND FORM OF THE SACRAMENT

The priest now pours baptismal water on the

BAPTISM

candidate's head thrice, each time in the form of a cross, saying once:

N, I baptise you in the name of + the Father, and of + the Son, and of + the Holy Spirit.
R. Amen.

If the baptism is conditional, the priest says:

N, if you are not already baptised, I baptise you in the name of + the Father, and of + the Son, and of + the Holy Spirit.
R. Amen.

ANOINTING WITH THE HOLY CHRISM

The priest takes the Holy Chrism and anoints the baptised therewith, signing the cross upon the crown of the candidate's head where indicated and saying:

Almighty God, the Father of our Lord Jesus Christ, has regenerated you by water and the Holy Spirit, and has pardoned all your failings. May he himself anoint + you with saving Chrism in the same Christ Jesus our Lord, that you may know life eternal.

Peace be with you.
R. And with your spirit.

COME AND WORSHIP

5 - GLORY

THE WHITE GARMENT

The priest takes the white garment - a short white stole - and places it upon the baptised, saying:

Receive the white garment, symbol of the New Life into which you have entered, and token of that true spiritual vestment of purity and holiness in which you shall stand before the throne of the heavenly grace.
R. Amen.

THE SHINING LIGHT

A lighted lamp is presented to candidate or sponsor.

Receive this burning lamp, the symbol of the light of Christ which is within you, the light which enlightens you and gives light to others. In that true light may you find the holy of holies in which the eternal priest dwells. Preserve the beauty and promise of your baptism throughout your life. Faithfully keep God's commandments. So shall you be prepared, in company with all the holy ones, to meet the Lord in the courts of heaven when he comes as bridegroom to his marriage feast; and so shall you live for ever.
R. Amen.

VALEDICTION

Go in peace, *N*, and the Lord be with you.
R. Amen.

VISITATION

VISITATION OF THE SICK

For 1 and 2 below, a Votive Mass for the Sick may be celebrated, at any time prior to the visitation. For 3 below, a Votive Mass of The Precious Blood is suitable to be celebrated at any time prior to the Visitation.

1

VISITATION WITH ANOINTING AND COMMUNION

A small table, covered with a white cloth, is set in readiness in the invalid's room, and upon it is placed a crucifix between two lighted candles, a small bowl of ordinary water, a white napkin, and some cubes of ordinary bread.

Holy water, a pyx containing the consecrated host, a phial of Oleum Infirmorum, a violet stole and a white stole, are brought by the priest.

Entering into the invalid's room, the priest, wearing the violet stole, first says:

Peace be upon this house.
R. And upon all who dwell herein.

(If it is necessary, another person may speak for the invalid.)

The priest purifies the room with holy water, saying:

COME AND WORSHIP

Sprinkle me with hyssop, O Lord, and I shall be clean.
R. Wash me and I shall be whiter than snow.

The priest sprinkles the invalid with holy water, saying:

Embrace me with your love, O God.
R. According to your great and loving kindness.

Glory be to the Father and to the Son and to the Holy Spirit.
R. As it was in the beginning, is now, and ever shall be, world without end. Amen.

Sprinkle me with hyssop, O Lord, and I shall be clean.
R. Wash me and I shall be whiter than snow.

O Lord, pour forth your love upon us.
R. And grant us your salvation.

Lord, hear our prayer.
R. And let our cry come before you.

The Lord be with you.
R. And also with you.

Let us pray.

The priest now prays for God to send his heavenly guardian-messenger:

O Lord, holy One, omnipotent and eternal God, hear our prayer, and in your goodness send your holy angel from heaven, to watch over, to cherish and to protect, to abide with and to defend, all

VISITATION

who dwell in this house.
R. Amen.

Lord, have mercy.
R. Christ, have mercy.
Lord, have mercy.

Our Father who art in heaven, hallowed be thy name; thy kingdom come, thy will be done on earth as it is in heaven. Give us this day our daily bread; and forgive us our trespasses, as we forgive those who trespass against us. And lead us not into temptation, but deliver us from evil. Amen.

O holy Lord, fount of all grace and blessing: look upon your servant *N* with the eyes of your love, and stretch over him/her the mighty hand of your protection. Through Christ our Lord.
R. Amen.

The priest addresses the invalid.

N, Child of God, make now your confession.

The invalid, or the spokesperson for the invalid, says the general confession.

Gracious God, I come before you, trusting in your great and loving kindness.
I adore you.
My soul praises you and blesses your holy name.
For all my failings towards you, most loving Lord, towards my fellow human beings, and towards myself, I am truly repentant.
Hear me, O God of Truth.
I open my heart to you.

COME AND WORSHIP

I welcome the outpouring of your healing light, and with the aid of your grace I will walk henceforth in the paths of righteousness.

The priest pronounces the absolution:

May the almighty and loving Lord, the God of all mercy, grant you + forgiveness and perfect remission of your sins, time for amendment of life, and the grace and comfort of the Holy Spirit.
R. Amen.

O Saviour of the world, by your cross and precious blood you have redeemed us.
R. Save us and help us, we humbly pray you, O Lord.

The priest lays the right hand upon the head of the invalid, saying:

God most powerful, most loving, bestower of all health, helper of all who call upon your name: let the abundance of your loving kindness be poured forth upon your servant N, that being restored to wholeness and balance he/she may give thanks to you in your holy Church. Through Christ our Lord.
R. Amen.

The priest now anoints the head or forehead of the candidate with the sign of the cross, as indicated. As the priest says 'Let your healing light ...' the right hand may again be laid upon the invalid.

In the name and love of Christ, and by the mighty power of the Holy Spirit, + give lasting health of soul and body to this your servant, we entreat you, Lord. Let   your healing light flood into

VISITATION

him/her, let it move within him/her, let it pervade him/her through and through, restoring him/her to wholeness, and leading him/her to possess life in abundance.

The priest cleanses the thumb, assumes the white stole, and reverently opens the pyx. Holding up the host, the priest says:

Behold the Lamb of God, behold him who takes away the sins of the world.
R. Lord, I am not worthy to receive you, but only say the word and my soul shall be healed.

The priest gives the host to the invalid:

May the body of our Lord Jesus Christ preserve your soul in everlasting life.
R. Amen.

The lustration of the priest's fingers now takes place, and things are set in order as necessary.

The Lord be with you.
R. And with your spirit.

Let us pray.

Lord most holy, eternal and mighty God, we pray with faith that *N* may benefit by receiving the most holy body of our Lord Jesus Christ: to be healed, if such be your will, and to know inner strength and blessing. Through the same Christ our Lord, who lives and reigns with you and the Holy Spirit, one God, throughout all ages.
R. Amen.

COME AND WORSHIP

Unto God's loving kindness and protection we commit you. The Lord + bless you and keep you. The Lord make his face to shine upon you, and be gracious unto you. The Lord lift up his countenance upon you, and give you peace, now and evermore.
R. Amen.

2

VISITATION WITH ANOINTING

A small table, covered with a white cloth, is set in readiness in the invalid's room, and upon it is placed a crucifix between two lighted candles, a small bowl of ordinary water, a white napkin, and some cubes of ordinary bread.

Holy water, a phial of Oleum Infirmorum, and a violet stole, are brought by the priest.

Entering into the invalid's room, the priest, wearing the violet stole, first says:

Peace be upon this house.
R. And upon all who dwell herein.

The priest purifies the invalid and the room with holy water, saying:

Sprinkle me with hyssop, O Lord, and I shall be clean.
R. Wash me and I shall be whiter than snow.

O Christ our Lord, may unending happiness make here its dwelling, may all within this place know

VISITATION

divine prosperity, may serenity surround them, may fruitful charity abound, and may all within this place ever be well. Magnify your holy name upon us, O Lord, and + bless our words and our actions: you who are holy, you who are good, you who live with the Father in the unity of the Holy Spirit, throughout all ages.
R. Amen.

Bless this + dwelling, O Christ our Lord, and all who are within it. Send an angel from heaven to keep vigil, we pray you, to ward all harm from them, to dispel all disquiet, and to guard them securely: you who live and reign with the Father and the Holy Spirit, throughout all ages.
R. Amen.

The priest addresses the invalid.

N, Child of God, make now your confession.

The invalid, or the spokesperson, says the confession.

**I confess to almighty God,
the Father, the Son and the Holy Spirit,
that I have sinned in thought, word and deed,
through my own most grievous fault.
Wherefore I pray almighty God
to have mercy upon me,
to forgive me all my sins,
and to bring me to everlasting life.**

The priest pronounces the absolution:

May the almighty and loving Lord, the God of all mercy, grant you + forgiveness and perfect remission of your sins, time for amendment of

COME AND WORSHIP

life, and the grace and comfort of the Holy Spirit.

The priest lays the right hand upon the head of the invalid, saying:

God most powerful, most loving, bestower of all health, the help of all who call upon your name: let the abundance of your loving kindness be poured forth upon your servant N, that being restored to wholeness and balance he/she may give thanks to you in your holy Church. Through Christ our Lord.
R. Amen.

The priest now anoints the head or forehead of the candidate with the sign of the cross, as indicated. As the priest says 'Let your healing light ...' the right hand may again be laid upon the invalid.

In the name and love of Christ, and by the mighty power of the Holy Spirit, + give lasting health of soul and body to this your servant, we entreat you, Lord. Let your healing light flood into him/her, let it move within him/her, let it pervade him/her through and through, restoring him/her to wholeness, and leading him/her to possess life in abundance.

The priest cleanses the thumb.

Unto God's loving kindness and protection we commit you. The Lord + bless you and keep you. The Lord make his face to shine upon you, and be gracious unto you. The Lord lift up his countenance upon you, and give you peace, now and evermore.
R. Amen.

VISITATION

3

EXTREME UNCTION

A small table, covered with a white cloth, is set in readiness in the invalid's room, and upon it is placed a crucifix between two lighted candles, a small bowl of ordinary water, a white napkin, and some cubes of ordinary bread.

Holy water, a pyx containing the consecrated host, a phial of Oleum Infirmorum, a hand-held crucifix, a violet stole and a white stole, are brought by the priest.

Entering into the invalid's room, the priest, wearing the violet stole, first says:

Peace be upon this house.
R. And upon all who dwell herein.

The priest purifies the invalid with holy water, saying:

Sprinkle me with hyssop, O Lord, and I shall be clean.
R. Wash me and I shall be whiter than snow.

O Christ our Lord, magnify your holy name upon us, and + bless our words and our actions: you who are holy, you who are good, you who live with the Father in the unity of the Holy Spirit, throughout all ages.
R. Amen.

The priest presents the crucifix for the invalid to kiss, and then says:

COME AND WORSHIP

N, Child of God, make now your confession.

The invalid, or the spokesperson for the invalid, says the general confession. But if the invalid signifies a desire to make private and personal confession, the priest first listens to his or her words. At discretion, the general confession may be omitted. Absolution is not given at this point.

I confess to almighty God,
the Father, the Son and the Holy Spirit,
that I have sinned in thought, word and deed,
through my own most grievous fault.
Wherefore I pray almighty God
to have mercy upon me,
to forgive me all my sins,
and to bring me to everlasting life.

With right arm outstretched over the invalid, the priest blesses him or her as indicated, thereafter resting the right hand upon him or her:

In the name of the + Father, through the love of the + Son, and by the power of the + Holy Spirit, may all trace of unworthiness be extinguished in you. Amen.

The priest now anoints the invalid with the sign of the cross, as indicated, saying:

(While anointing the eyelids)

By this sacred unction + + and his most loving kindness may the Lord forgive you whatever you have failed in by the ability to see.

VISITATION

(While anointing the ears)

By this sacred unction + + and his most loving kindness may the Lord forgive you whatever you have failed in by the ability to hear.

(While anointing the nostrils)

By this sacred unction + + and his most loving kindness may the Lord forgive you whatever you have failed in by the ability to smell.

(While anointing the closed mouth)

By this sacred unction + and his most loving kindness may the Lord forgive you whatever you have failed in by the ability to taste and the ability to speak.

(While anointing the hands)

By this sacred unction + + and his most loving kindness may the Lord forgive you whatever you have failed in by the ability to touch.

(While anointing the feet)

By this sacred unction + + and his most loving kindness may the Lord forgive you whatever you have failed in by the ability to walk.

The priest pronounces absolution.

May the almighty and loving Lord grant you pardon, absolution and remission of your sins. Amen.

COME AND WORSHIP

By the power vested in me, and with authority from Christ, I absolve you from your sins, in the name of the Father, and of the + Son, and of the Holy Spirit. Amen.

The priest cleanses his hands. The bread that is used is afterwards to be burned, as convenient.

Let us pray.

O Christ, our redeemer, by the grace of the Holy Spirit restore N to health, in body and soul, we entreat you, that he/she may be made whole. Let the light and fire of the Holy Spirit course through him/her and about him/her, to purify him/her, to renew him/her, and to bring to him/her strength and blessing: you who reign with the Father and the same Holy Spirit, throughout all ages.
R. Amen.

Stretch forth the right hand of your power, O God most holy, most mighty; strengthen your servant; restore him/her to your Church, and equip him/her with all that he/she requires in order to prosper. Through Christ our Lord.
R. Amen.

The priest assumes the white stole, reverently opens the pyx, and holds up the host, saying:

Behold the Lamb of God, behold him who takes away the sins of the world.

The priest gives the host to the invalid:

N, my brother/sister, receive the viaticum, the food for your journey, the body of our Lord Jesus

VISITATION

Christ: he who will keep you in perfect safety and guide you to eternal life. Amen.

The lustration of the priest's fingers now takes place, and things are set in order as necessary.

The Lord be with you.
R. And with your spirit.

Let us pray.

Lord most holy, eternal and mighty God, we pray with faith that *N* may benefit by receiving the most holy body of our Lord Jesus Christ: to be healed, if such be your will, and to know inner strength and blessing. Through the same Christ our Lord, who lives and reigns with you and the Holy Spirit, one God, throughout all ages.
R. Amen.

Most loving God, look with kindness upon your servant *N*, whose true faith and Christian hope commend him/her. Visit him/her with your salvation. Free your servant from all failings through the passion and death of your only Son. Of your loving kindness forgive and pardon him/her, that his/her soul, in the hour of its leaving, may find in you a merciful judge; and being made clean in the blood of your Son may be worthy to pass to life eternal. Through the same Christ our Lord.
R. Amen.

May almighty God bless you: the Father, and the + Son, and the Holy Spirit,
R. Amen.

COME AND WORSHIP

4

EXTREME UNCTION

In case of necessity, there being little time left to the invalid, the rite of Extreme Unction may be conducted simply, as follows:

The priest addresses the invalid:

Do you love God?

The invalid having given answer, the priest continues:

Are you truly sorry for all your sins?

If the invalid is beyond speech, the priest omits the foregoing questions, and encourages him or her to turn his or her thoughts to God: in repentance, and in loving trust.

The priest anoints the brow of the invalid with the sign of the cross as indicated, saying:

By this sacred unction + and his most loving kindness, may the Lord forgive you whatever you have failed in by thought, word or deed.

The priest pronounces the absolution:

By the power vested in me, and with authority from Christ, I absolve you from your sins, in the name of the Father, and of the + Son, and of the Holy Spirit. Amen.

The invalid receives viaticum. If necessary, a fragment of the host may be given with a little wine or water.

VISITATION

My brother/sister, receive the viaticum, the food for your journey, the body of our Lord Jesus Christ: he who will keep you in perfect safety and guide you to eternal life. Amen.

The priest continues:

By the most holy mysteries of the redemption, may God, the loving and most mighty, deliver you and regenerate you; may he open the gates of paradise to you, and lead you into unending joy.
R. Amen.

May almighty God bless you: the Father, and the + Son, and the Holy Spirit.
R. Amen.

5

FINAL ABSOLUTION

If the priest is called to a person who is at the point of death, at necessity the following formula may be used.

I absolve you from all your failings, in the name of the Father, and of the + Son, and of the Holy Spirit. Amen.

COME AND WORSHIP

CONFESSION

The act of auricular confession is encouraged as a spiritual discipline and as an act of inner purification; it is likewise a means for the restoration of the harmony, the balance, that exists between the individual soul and the Creator.

Before making confession to the priest, meditate and pray in quietness, looking within yourself, honestly considering anything in which you feel that you have failed, anything in which you feel you have not met the standards necessary to human dignity and honour, or the standards required by the precepts of God.

When appropriate, say the first part of the general confession, as follows:

I confess to almighty God,
the Father, the Son, and the Holy Spirit,
that I have sinned in thought, word and deed,
through my own most grievous fault.

Enter now to the priest, and say:

Bless me, father/mother, for I have sinned.

As the priest blesses you, make the sign of the cross upon yourself.

Speak without formality, making your confession as your heart guides you and as your conscience requires. Remember that the priest represents the Lord Christ: speak then, to the priest, as to that most holy, most precious and most understanding of friends.

181

CONFESSION

When you have finished your confession, say:

This is my confession, wherein I have drawn aside the veils of mind and heart, that healing light may enter the inner chamber of my being.

Now conclude the confiteor:

Wherefore I pray almighty God to have mercy upon me,
to forgive me all my sins,
and to bring me to everlasting life.

Before granting you absolution, the priest may offer you guidance or reassurance, or may discuss with you matters arising from your confession.

The priest then says:

May the almighty and loving Lord grant you pardon, absolution and remission of your sins. Amen.

By the power vested in me, and with authority from Christ, I absolve you from your sins, in the name of the Father, and of the + Son, and of the Holy Spirit. Amen.

When you leave the priest, again meditate and pray in quietness, knowing that your sins have been absolved, and that God's healing power and grace are at work within you: and in this wonderful knowledge, with this promise of light restored and life renewed, look within, and in love of God truly and completely forgive yourself.

COME AND WORSHIP

THE FUNERAL RITE

This rite may be conducted with or without Mass, the following provisions applying:

If Requiem Mass is to be said, Part I, the Reception, takes place in the Church; Part II, the Requiem Mass itself, is celebrated likewise in the Church. If burial has been chosen, then the ceremony proceeds from Part II to Part III, which takes place in the cemetery; while if cremation has been chosen, the rite omits Part III and proceeds from Part II to Part IV, which takes place in the chapel of the crematorium.

If there is no Requiem Mass, Part I may be conducted in the Church. If burial has been chosen, then the rite omits Part II and proceeds from Part I to Part III, which takes place in the cemetery; while if cremation has been chosen, the rite omits Part II and Part III and proceeds from Part I to Part IV, which takes place in the chapel of the crematorium.

Again, there being no Requiem Mass, for both burial and cremation Part I may be conducted in the chapel of the crematorium; then, in the case of burial, the rite proceeds from Part I to Part III, which takes place in the cemetery; while, in the case of cremation, the rite proceeds from Part I to Part IV, and continues within the chapel of the crematorium.

The choice of songs or of live or recorded music, and the actual place of song or music within this rite, is left entirely flexible, thus to accord with the discretion of the priest and the desires of the mourners.

FUNERAL RITES

PART I

RECEPTION OF THE BODY

The deceased is brought to the entrance of the Church or of the Chapel, to be met by the priest, who sprinkles the coffin with holy water. Then the coffin is escorted to its place, the priest saying these verses:

Out of the depths have I cried unto you, O Lord: Lord hear my voice.
Let your ears be attentive: to the voice of my supplications.
If you, O Lord, should mark iniquities: O Lord, who shall bear it?
But there is forgiveness with you: that you may be held in reverence.
I wait for the Lord, my soul waits: and in the Lord's word is my hope.
My soul waits for the Lord, more than watchmen for the morning: more, I say, than those who watch for the morning.
Let Israel hope in the Lord: for with the Lord is mercy, and fullness of redemption.
God shall redeem Israel: from all iniquity.
Glory be to the Father, and to the Son: and to the Holy Spirit.
As it was in the beginning, is now, and ever shall be: world without end Amen.

When the coffin is in its place the priest continues:

Saints of God, come to his/her aid; all you angels of the Lord, greet him/her.
Receive his/her soul and offer it in the sight of the Most High.

COME AND WORSHIP

O Christ, you who called him/her: receive him/her unto yourself.
O you angels of light, lead him/her into the bosom of Abraham
Receive his/her soul and offer it in the sight of the Most High.
Rest eternal grant unto him/her, O Lord, and let light perpetual shine upon him/her.

Lord have mercy.
R. Lord have mercy.
Christ have mercy.
R. Christ have mercy.
Lord have mercy.
R. Lord have mercy.

All say together:

Our Father who art in heaven, hallowed be thy name; thy kingdom come, thy will be done on earth as it is in heaven. Give us this day our daily bread; and forgive us our trespasses, as we forgive those who trespass against us. And lead us not into temptation, but deliver us from evil. Amen.

The priest continues:

O Lord, by your great and loving kindness, absolve the soul of *N* from all bonds of sin; that he/she may have life and breath in the glory of the resurrection, in company with all your saints and holy ones. Through Jesus Christ your Son, our Lord, who lives and reigns with you in the unity of the Holy Spirit, one God, throughout all ages.
R. Amen.

FUNERAL RITES

(Funeral without Mass)

If Mass is not to be celebrated, one or more of the following readings are now used, or other readings may be chosen. But John 14: 1-6 shall always be used.

1 Peter 1: 3-9
Revelation 22: 1-5
John 11: 21-27
John 14: 1-6

An address or eulogy is here delivered; and then, omitting Mass, the service proceeds to the Committal, Part III or Part IV as appropriate, as below.

(Funeral with Mass)

If Mass is to be celebrated, the following order is to be observed, with the service proceeding to the Requiem Mass of Part II, provisions for which are given immediately below.

PART II

THE REQUIEM MASS

The Requiem Mass commences with the Proper Introit, which is said or sung:

Rest eternal grant unto them, O Lord, and let light perpetual shine upon them.
To you, O God, a hymn of praise is due in Sion, and unto you will the vow be performed in Jerusalem. O you that hear my prayer, unto you shall all flesh come.

COME AND WORSHIP

Glory be to the Father, and to the Son, and to the Holy Spirit. As it was in the beginning, is now, and ever shall be, world without end. Amen.
Rest eternal grant unto them, O Lord, and let light perpetual shine upon them.

Kyrie and Gloria are omitted, and the Collect is said.

The following Collect may be used, or that which is ordinarily provided for Funeral Mass (pages 300-301).

O you, who are the Life Eternal, which was with the Father and the Holy Spirit and was manifested to us; you, who by your coming in light bestowed life and immortality; we pray you in this hour of sorrow to deliver us from the shadows which encompass us, that we may be enabled to behold clearly the shining of your countenance and the reality of your gracious purpose. Of your loving kindness, keep safely the life of *N* that, for a time, is lost to us. May he/she dwell now within the temple of your holiness, to await the day when your perfect glory shall be revealed and we shall all, in innocence and joy, dwell in your presence evermore: O you, who live and reign with the Father in the unity of the Holy Spirit, one God throughout all ages.

Epistle: Revelation 22: 1-5
Gospel: John 14: 1-6

The Affirmation of Faith is omitted.

An address, or eulogy, may here be delivered.

The text at the beginning of the Offertory is:

FUNERAL RITES

Lord Jesus Christ, King of Glory, may your holy angel and standard-bearer blessed Michael bring the souls of all the faithful departed into your holy light.

If Agnus Dei forms part of the rite, the words are:

O Lamb of God, you take away the sins of the world: grant them rest.

O Lamb of God, you take away the sins of the World: grant them rest.

O Lamb of God, you take away the sins of the world: grant them eternal rest.

The blessing at the end of Mass is omitted.

The celebrant stands before the coffin and says:

Enter not into judgment with your servant, O Lord, but grant perfect remission of his/her sins. In your great loving kindness, pass no weighty sentence on him/her, whose true faith and prayers commend him/her to you. May your grace enfold him/her, and bring him/her to your light, for in life he/she was sealed with the sign of the Holy Trinity: you who live and reign throughout all ages.
R. Amen.

The celebrant sprinkles the coffin with holy water.

PART III

THE COMMITTAL

COME AND WORSHIP

(Burial)

The coffin is escorted from Church or Chapel to the intended place of burial, the following being meanwhile said or sung:

The Lord is my shepherd: I shall not want.
He makes me to lie down in green pastures: he leads me beside the still waters.
He restores my soul: he leads me in the paths of righteousness for his name's sake.
Yea, though I walk through the valley of the shadow of death, I will fear no ill: for you are with me, your rod and your staff they comfort me.
You prepare a table before me in the presence of my enemies: you anoint my head with oil, my cup overflows.
Surely goodness and love shall follow me all the days of my life: and I will dwell in the house of the Lord for ever.

If the grave is to be blessed, the priest now blesses it, and the coffin and the grave are sprinkled with holy water. If the grave has been blessed, the coffin is sprinkled with holy water. The priest says:

I am the Resurrection and the Life, says the Lord. Those who believe in me, though they die, yet shall they live. And those who live and believe in me shall never die.

Blessed are those who die in the Lord; even so, says the Spirit, for they rest from their labours. And God shall wipe all tears from their eyes; and there shall be no more death, neither sorrow, nor crying, neither shall there be any more pain: for the former things are passed away.

FUNERAL RITES

The coffin is sprinkled with holy water by the priest.
May the soul of our departed brother/sister rest in peace.
R. Amen.

O Lord, hear my prayer.
R. And let my cry come before you.

The Lord be with you.
R. And with your spirit.

Let us pray.

Almighty God, with whom live the spirits of those who depart hence in the Lord, and with whom the souls of the faithful, after they are delivered from the body, are in joy and blessedness; we pray you to hasten your kingdom, that we, with all those who are departed in the true faith of your Holy Name, may find perfect consummation and bliss in the eternal and everlasting glory. Through Christ our Lord.
R. Amen.

Rest eternal grant unto him/her, O Lord.
R. And let light perpetual shine upon him/her.

Sprinkling a little earth upon the coffin at the appropriate moment, the priest says:

Forasmuch as it has pleased almighty God of his great mercy to take to himself the soul of our brother/sister here departed, we therefore commit his/her body to the ground, earth to earth, ashes to ashes, dust to dust: but the spirit returns to God, from whom it came forth.

COME AND WORSHIP

Let us pray.

Eternal God, Lord of life, we thank you for the hope, sure and certain, of the life everlasting. We sorrow not as those without hope. And yet, O our God, regard us with your kindness if, sorrowing, our hearts linger over life's long and last farewells, and if, in our grief at the passing of faces we shall not again see on earth, we find it hard to say: The Lord has given and the Lord has taken away; blessed be the name of the Lord. Yet in faith we say, Now and evermore, blessed be your name.
R. Amen.

For the gift of your servant *N* we praise you. For the memory of word and deed which quickens our hearts and sanctifies, we praise you. Let there be no bitterness in our sorrow, no unbelief. Set your star above our darkness, and let it shine until the day breaks. We ask this in the name of the risen Christ.
R. Amen.

The righteous live for ever, and the care of them is with the Most High. The right hand of God shall cover them; the arm of God shall be their shield.

May almighty God bless you, the Father, and + the Son, and the Holy Spirit.
R. Amen.

PART IV

THE COMMITTAL

FUNERAL RITES

(Cremation)

If Part I, or Parts I or II, were conducted in the Church, the priest meets the coffin at the entrance to the chapel of the crematorium and escorts it to its place of repose, saying the following verses.

But if the funeral was begun in the chapel of the crematorium, the coffin will already be in its place of repose, and the priest continues the rite, saying:

I am the Resurrection and the Life, says the Lord. Those who believe in me, though they die, yet shall they live. And those who live and believe in me shall never die.

Blessed are those who die in the Lord; even so, says the Spirit, for they rest from their labours.

And God shall wipe all tears from their eyes; and there shall be no more death, neither sorrow, nor crying, neither shall there be any more pain: for the former things are passed away.

The coffin is sprinkled with holy water by the priest.

May the soul of our departed brother/sister rest in peace.
R. Amen.

O Lord, hear my prayer.
R. And let my cry come before you.

The Lord be with you.
R. And with your spirit.

COME AND WORSHIP

Let us pray.

Almighty God, with whom live the spirits of those who depart hence in the Lord, and with whom the souls of the faithful, after they are delivered from the body, are in joy and blessedness; we pray you to hasten your kingdom, that we, with all those who are departed in the true faith of your Holy Name, may find perfect consummation and bliss in the eternal and everlasting glory. Through Christ our Lord.
R. Amen.

Rest eternal grant unto him/her, O Lord.
R. And let light perpetual shine upon him/her.

The coffin now departs from the assembly, while the priest says:

Forasmuch as it has pleased almighty God of his great mercy to take to himself the soul of our brother/sister here departed, we therefore commit his/her body to the flame: but the spirit returns to God, from whom it came forth.

Let us pray.

Eternal God, Lord of life, we thank you for the hope, sure and certain, of the life everlasting. We sorrow not as those without hope. And yet, O our God, regard us with your kindness if, sorrowing, our hearts linger over life's long and last farewells, and if, in our grief at the passing of faces we shall not again see on earth, we find it hard to say: The Lord has given and the Lord has taken away; blessed be the name of the Lord. Yet

FUNERAL RITES

in faith we say, Now and evermore, blessed be
your name.
R. Amen.

For the gift of your servant *N* we praise you. For
the memory of word and deed which quickens our
hearts and sanctifies, we praise you. Let there be
no bitterness in our sorrow, no unbelief. Set your
star above our darkness, and let it shine until the
day breaks. We ask this in the name of the risen
Christ.
R. Amen.

The righteous live for ever, and the care of them
is with the Most High. The right hand of God shall
cover them; the arm of God shall be their shield.

May almighty God bless you: the Father, and + the
Son, and the Holy Spirit.
R. Amen.

Collects & Readings

COME AND WORSHIP

COLLECTS & READINGS

TEMPORAL CYCLE

ADVENT

First Sunday of Advent

Come, O Lord, in your strength; come, be our defender against the works of darkness that surround us; come, O Lord, in your mercy, and be our redeemer to bring us salvation: you who live and reign with God the Father in the unity of the Holy Spirit, one God, throughout all ages.

Epistle: Romans 13: 11-14
Gospel: Luke 21: 25-33

Second Sunday of Advent

Stir our hearts, O Lord, to make ready the ways of your only Son, that, with minds purified by his coming, we may serve you and glorify your holy name. Through the same Jesus Christ your Son, our Lord, who lives and reigns with you in the unity of the Holy Spirit, one God, throughout all ages.

Epistle: Romans 15: 4-13
Gospel: Matthew 11: 2-10

COLLECTS AND READINGS

Third Sunday of Advent

Hear our prayer, O Lord, and by the grace of your coming illumine our hearts and our minds, that we may both know and feel the power of your love within us: you who live and reign with God the Father in the unity of the Holy Spirit, one God, throughout all ages.

Epistle: Philippians 4: 4-7
Gospel: John 1: 19-28

Fourth Sunday of Advent

Arise in your power, O Lord: come among us, and support us with your strength; and let your abundant grace and your great loving kindness help us and deliver us, through the mediation of your Son our Lord, to whom with you and the Holy Spirit be all honour and glory, throughout all ages.

Epistle:1 Corinthians 4: 1-5
Gospel: Luke 3: 1-6

Eve of the Nativity

Loving God, as we turn our thoughts to our redemption, our souls are filled with gladness. When your only Son comes as judge, may we receive him as joyfully as we now receive him as redeemer. Through Christ our Lord.

Epistle: Romans 1: 1-6
Gospel: Matthew 1: 18-21

NATIVITY

Feast of the Nativity

Midnight Mass

O Lord, God of glory, you have made this most holy night to shine with the radiance of the true light. May we come to know the mystery of this light on earth, and may we be received into its glorious splendour in heaven. Through Christ our Lord.

Epistle: Titus 2: 11-15
Gospel: Luke 2: 1-14

Dawn Mass

God of all power, God of all majesty, we are bathed in the new light of the incarnate Word. May this light, shining in our minds by faith, shine also in our deeds. Through Christ our Lord.

Epistle: Titus 3: 4-7
Gospel: Luke 2: 15-20

Daytime Mass

Most mighty God, may the incarnation of your only Son bring redemption to all people, freeing them from the ancient bondage of sin and bringing them into your wonderful light. Through the same Christ our Lord.

Epistle: Hebrews 1: 1-12
Gospel: John 1: 1-14

COLLECTS AND READINGS

First Sunday of Nativity

Within the Octave of Nativity

Almighty God, direct our lives in harmony with your will, we pray you, that we may excel in righteousness, and perform worthy deeds in the name of your beloved Son. Through the same Jesus Christ your only Son, our Lord, who lives and reigns with you in the unity of the Holy Spirit, one God, throughout all ages.

Epistle: Galatians 4: 1-7
Gospel: Luke 2: 33-40

Octave of Nativity (if Sunday): The Holy Name

O God, you established your only Son as the Saviour of humankind, and you decreed that he should be called Jesus: graciously grant us, we pray you, that our reverence for his holy name on earth may lead to our adoration of his countenance in heaven. Through the same Jesus Christ our Lord, who lives and reigns with you and the Holy Spirit, one God, throughout all ages.

Epistle: Acts 4: 8-12
Gospel: Luke 2: 21

Second Sunday of Nativity

Most powerful God, you wonderfully created us in your own image, and yet more wonderfully restored us: grant, we pray you, that we may come to share in the divinity of him who deigned to share our humanity, Jesus Christ, your Son, our

COME AND WORSHIP

Lord, who lives and reigns with you and the Holy Spirit, one God, throughout all ages.

Epistle: 2 Corinthians 8: 9
Gospel: John 1: 14-18

EPIPHANY

Feast of the Epiphany

O God, you revealed your son this day to all the peoples of the earth by the guiding of a star: grant, we pray you, that we who know you now by faith, may be led to the presence of your celestial splendour. Through the same Jesus Christ your Son, our Lord, who lives and reigns with you and the Holy Spirit, one God, throughout all ages.

Lesson: Isaiah 60: 1-6
Gospel: Matthew 2: 1-12

First Sunday after Epiphany

O Lord our God, be pleased to receive the prayers of your people who call upon you, and graciously grant that we may clearly discern the things we ought to do, and be empowered to accomplish them faithfully. Through Jesus Christ your Son, our Lord, who lives and reigns with you and the Holy Spirit, one God, throughout all ages.

Epistle: Romans 12: 1-5
Gospel: Luke 2: 41-52

COLLECTS AND READINGS

Second Sunday after Epiphany

All-powerful and everlasting God, ruler of all things in the heavens and upon earth, in your goodness hear our prayers, and grant peace in our time. Through Christ our Lord.
Epistle: Romans 12: 6-16
Gospel: John 2: 1-11

Third Sunday after Epiphany

All-powerful and everlasting God, in your great and loving kindness look upon our weakness, and in all our dangers and necessities stretch forth the right hand of your power to aid us and defend us. Through Jesus Christ our Lord, who lives and reigns with you and the Holy Spirit, one God, throughout all ages.

Epistle: Romans 12: 16-21
Gospel: Matthew 8: 1-13

Fourth Sunday after Epiphany

O God, it is with your aid that we are able to stand firm among the many and great dangers, material and spiritual, that beset us in this life: therefore, we pray you, keep us always in wholeness of mind and body, perfectly attuned to your will, so that in your name we may triumph over all adversity. Through Christ our Lord.

Epistle: Romans 13: 8-10
Gospel: Matthew 8: 23-27

COME AND WORSHIP

Fifth Sunday after Epiphany

O Lord, watch over your household, that it may ever be secure in your loving protection: defended by your mighty power and continually aspiring to celestial grace. Through Christ our Lord.

Epistle: Colossians 3: 12-17
Gospel: Matthew 13: 24-30

Sixth Sunday after Epiphany

All-powerful God, whose blessed and only Son was manifested that he might redeem the world and make us your children and heirs of everlasting life, graciously grant that our minds being ever stirred to noble aspiration, we may purify ourselves, even as he is pure; that when he comes again we may be made like unto him in his glorious kingdom; where with you, O Father, and you, O Holy Spirit, he lives and reigns, one God, throughout all ages.

Epistle: 1 John 3: 1-8
Gospel: Matthew 24: 23-31

TIME BEFORE LENT

Septuagesima

From today until Easter, Gloria in Excelsis is not said.

Gracious Lord, hear the cry of your people: deliver us, most mighty, by your great and loving kindness, that we may be regenerated in holy light to the glory of your name. Through Jesus Christ

COLLECTS AND READINGS

your Son, our Lord, who lives and reigns with you and the Holy Spirit, one God, throughout all ages.

Epistle: 1 Corinthians 9: 24-27, 10: 1-5
Gospel: Matthew 20: 1-16

Sexagesima

Most mighty God, you are our strength and our rock: grant that we may ever dwell within the shield of your defence, secure from all adversity. Through Jesus Christ your Son, our Lord, who lives and reigns with you and the Holy Spirit, one God, throughout all ages.

Epistle: 2 Corinthians 11: 19-31
Gospel: Luke 8: 4-15

Quinquagesima

O Lord, you have taught us that without love all our deeds are of no value: send your Holy Spirit, we pray you, and pour into our hearts that most wonderful gift of love, the very bond of peace and of all virtues, without which gift we have no true life. Through Christ our Lord.

Epistle: 1 Corinthians 13: 1-13
Gospel: Luke 18: 31-43

LENT

Ash Wednesday

O Lord, may your faithful people begin this solemn fast in true piety, and continue it with unfailing

COME AND WORSHIP

devotion, that, acknowledging our failings, we may receive from you, God most loving, perfect remission and renewal. Through Christ our Lord.

Epistle: Joel 2: 12-19
Gospel: Matthew 6: 16-21

First Sunday of Lent

O God, in every year you purify your Church by the Lenten observance: grant to your whole household, we pray you, grace to use this abstinence rightly, that our minds and bodies being opened to true holiness we may be fruitful in good works, to your honour and glory. Through Jesus Christ your Son, our Lord, who lives and reigns with you and the Holy Spirit, one God, throughout all ages.

Epistle: 2 Corinthians 6: 1-10
Gospel: Matthew 4: 1-11

Second Sunday of Lent

Most mighty God, we rely always on your aid: keep us in holiness and harmony, we pray you, in our bodies and in our souls, that we may be defended from all physical adversities which may beset the body and from all negative influences which may affect the soul. Through Jesus Christ your Son, our Lord, who lives and reigns with you and the Holy Spirit, one God, throughout all ages.

Epistle: 1 Thessalonians 4: 1-7
Gospel: Matthew 15: 21-28

COLLECTS AND READINGS

Third Sunday of Lent

God of all majesty, look upon the devotion of your people; stretch forth the right hand of your power to defend us, fill us with your light that we may walk safely in knowledge of you. Through Jesus Christ your Son, our Lord, who lives and reigns with you and the Holy Spirit, one God, throughout all ages.

Epistle: Ephesians 5: 1-9
Gospel: Luke 11: 14-28

Fourth Sunday of Lent

God most mighty, grant that we who seek to live according to your commandments may be strengthened by the consolation of your grace. Through Jesus Christ your Son, our Lord, who lives and reigns with you and the Holy Spirit, one God, throughout all ages.

Epistle: Hebrews 12: 22-24
Gospel: John 6: 1-15

Fifth Sunday of Lent (Passion Sunday)

Almighty God, look with love upon your people, that by your great goodness they may be governed and protected in body and soul. Through Jesus Christ your Son, our Lord, who lives and reigns with you and the Holy Spirit, one God, throughout all ages.

Epistle: Hebrews 9: 11-15
Gospel: John 8: 46-59

COME AND WORSHIP

Sixth Sunday of Lent (Palm Sunday)

Blessing and Distribution of Palms

Red vestments are worn.

The Antiphon is said or sung:

Hosanna to the Son of David!
Blessed is he who comes in the name of the Lord,
the king of Israel.
Hosanna in excelsis!

The Lord be with you
R. And with your spirit.

Be pleased, O Lord, to + bless these branches,
which are to be borne in your honour. May our
earthly reverence on this day find fulfillment in
our souls, by our devotion to your work of
salvation. Through Jesus Christ your Son, our Lord,
who lives and reigns with you and the Holy Spirit,
one God, throughout all ages.

*The palms are sprinkled with holy water, and then
censed; after which they are distributed.*

*Psalm 24 is then said or chanted, preceded by the
Antiphon:*

Hosanna to the Son of David!
Blessed is he who comes in the name of the Lord,
the king of Israel.
Hosanna in excelsis!

The earth is the Lord's and the fullness thereof:
the world and they that dwell therein.

COLLECTS AND READINGS

For he has founded it upon the seas: and established it upon the floods.

Who shall ascend into the hill of the Lord: or who shall stand in his holy place?

He that has clean hands and a pure heart: who has not lifted up his soul to vanity, nor sworn deceitfully.

He shall receive the blessing from the Lord: and righteousness from the God of his salvation.

This is the generation of those who seek him: that seek your face, O Jacob.

Lift up your heads, O you gates, and be you lifted up, you everlasting doors: and the king of glory shall come in.

Who is this king of glory?: the Lord strong and mighty, the Lord mighty in battle.

Lift up your heads, O you gates, even lift them up, you everlasting doors: and the king of glory shall come in.

Who is this king of glory?: the Lord of hosts, he is the king of glory.

Glory be to the Father, and to the Son: and to the Holy Spirit.

As it was in the beginning, is now, and ever shall be: world without end. Amen.

The Antiphon is repeated:

Hosanna to the Son of David!
Blessed is he who comes in the name of the Lord, the king of Israel.
Hosanna in excelsis!

The following Gospel text is read by celebrant or by deacon:

COME AND WORSHIP

Gospel: Matthew 21: 1-9

The procession now takes place, led by the celebrant, the faithful bearing palms. The hymn 'Gloria, laus, et honor' is sung as the procession begins:

The Lord be with you.
R. And with your spirit.

Let us proceed in peace.
R. In the name of Christ. Amen.

All glory, laud and honour to thee, Redeemer, King,
To whom the lips of children made sweet hosannas ring.

Thou art the King of Israel, thou David's royal Son,
Who in the Lord's name comest, the King and blessed One.

All glory, laud and honour to thee, Redeemer, King,
To whom the lips of children made sweet hosannas ring.

The company of angels is praising thee on high,
And mortal folk and all things created make reply.

All glory, laud and honour to thee, Redeemer, King,
To whom the lips of children made sweet hosannas ring.

The people of the Hebrews with palms before thee went;

COLLECTS AND READINGS

Our praise and prayer and anthems before thee
we present.
All glory, laud and honour to thee, Redeemer,
King,
To whom the lips of children made sweet
hosannas ring.

To thee before thy passion they sang their hymns
of praise,
To thee, now high exalted, our melody we raise.

All glory, laud and honour to thee, Redeemer,
King,
To whom the lips of children made sweet
hosannas ring.

Thou didst accept their praises, accept the
prayers we bring,
Who in all good delightest, thou good and faithful
King.

All glory, laud and honour to thee, Redeemer,
King,
To whom the lips of children made sweet
hosannas ring.

Tr. John Mason Neale, 1818-66.

*The priest, on arriving at the altar, turns to face the
people, and says:*

The Lord be with you.
R. And with your spirit.

Let us pray.

COME AND WORSHIP

Lord Jesus Christ, our King and our Redeemer: bearing green branches, we have sung these praises in your honour. Wherever these branches are taken, may the grace of your blessing descend; so shall darkness and deceit depart, and your protecting hand be with those you have redeemed; O you who live and reign with God the Father in the unity of the Holy Spirit, one God, throughout all ages.
R. Amen.

The Mass of Palm Sunday

Violet vestments are worn.

Most mighty and eternal God, because of your so great love for all people, you sent your only Son, our Saviour Jesus Christ, to be born in this world, and to suffer death upon the cross, that we might follow the example of his great humility. Of your loving-kindness grant, we pray you, that we may both imitate his humility and have part in his resurrection. Through the same Jesus Christ your Son, our Lord, who lives and reigns with you and the Holy Spirit, one God, throughout all ages.

Epistle: Philippians 2: 5-11
Gospel: Matthew 27: 1-54

Monday in Holy Week

O God, in our weakness we are subject to adversity: grant, we pray you, that drawing life and strength from the passion of your Son we may be enabled to transcend our weakness and stand firm against all affliction. Through the same Jesus

COLLECTS AND READINGS

Christ your Son, our Lord, who lives and reigns with you and the Holy Spirit, one God, throughout all ages.

Reading: Isaiah 50: 5-10
Gospel: Mark 14: 1-72

Tuesday in Holy Week

Almighty and eternal God, grant us so to enter into the mysteries of our Lord's passion, that they may be re-enacted within our minds and souls: that the reality and depth of your love may rejoice within our hearts. Through the same Jesus Christ your Son, our Lord, who lives and reigns with you and the Holy Spirit, one God, throughout all ages.

Reading: Isaiah 63: 1-19
Gospel: Mark 15: 1-38

Wednesday in Holy Week

God of power, may the passion of your only Son free us from the night-time of sin and lead us to the morning of new life. Through the same Jesus Christ your Son, our Lord, who lives and reigns with you and the Holy Spirit, one God, throughout all ages.

Reading: Isaiah 53: 1-12
Gospel: Luke 22: 39-71, 23: 1-53

Maundy Thursday

Morning Mass of Chrism

COME AND WORSHIP

O Lord our God, in the abundance of your love you give New Life to your people through the agency of our priestly ministry; grant, therefore, we pray you, that we may ever rightly honour you in accordance with your will, and that in our day we may see your dedicated people increase in virtue by the gift of your grace. Through Jesus Christ our Lord, who lives and reigns with you and the Holy Spirit, one God, throughout all ages.

Reading: Isaiah 61: 1-9
Gospel: Luke 4: 16-22

At the Offertory, the ministers process to the sanctuary carrying the oils which are to be blessed. They are presented to the bishop and then placed on the prepared table, one by one.

The Chrism is presented by a minister, who says:

The Oil for Holy Chrism.

The oil is placed on the prepared table, and the Oil for Catechumens is presented by a minister, who says:

The Oil of Catechumens.

The oil is placed next to the oil for Chrism, and the Oil for the Infirm is presented by a minster, who says:

The Oil of the Infirm.

The oil is placed to the other side of the Chrism; and then the bread and wine are prepared.

At the conclusion of the Eucharistic Prayer of Consecration, before 'Through him, with him, etc' is

COLLECTS AND READINGS

*said in Rites 1 and 2, or before 'It is through him, etc'
in Rite 3, the Oil for the Infirm is brought to the
bishop and held before him at the altar.*

The bishop exorcizes the oil:

Creature of oil, I exorcize you that you may be
free from all powers of hindrance and malignity,
in the name of the + Father, and of the + Son, and
of the Holy + Spirit; that you may be an unction of
the spirit, to confirm that the Holy Spirit may
dwell within the body as in a temple of the Living
God.
R. Amen.

The blessing of the oil now takes place:

The Lord be with you.
R. And with your spirit.

Let us pray.

Send forth from heaven, we pray you, O Lord,
your Holy Spirit, the Paraclete, upon this oil,
which you have been pleased to bring forth from a
green tree to refresh soul and body. May your holy
blessing + rest upon this oil, that whosoever is
anointed with it may find therein a heavenly
medicine for soul and body, to drive away all
sorrows and infirmities. Let it be a perfect
anointing for us, a token of your blessing,
enduring forever within the heart of our being. In
the name of our Lord Jesus Christ.
R. Amen.

*The bishop continues with the final words of the
Eucharistic Prayer of Consecration, and the minister*

COME AND WORSHIP

returns the blessed Oil of the Infirm to its place.

After the Communion and the Ablutions, the blessing of the Chrism takes place. The bishop goes to the table, to stand facing the faithful. The priests form a semi-circle on his left and right, and the deacons stand behind him.

The bishop first blesses the balm which is to be added to the oil.

The Lord be with you.
R. And with your spirit.

Let us pray.

O God, preparer of all the celestial mysteries and their virtues, graciously hear our prayer. Upon this fragrant balm, produced from the tears shed by a noble tree, bestow your holy + blessing, that it may be an acceptable vehicle of your mysteries to enrich us with priestly anointing.
R. Amen.

The balm is blended with the oil.

Let us pray to the Lord our God most mighty, who wonderfully united our humanity with the illimitable godhead of his co-eternal Son. With the co-operation of the Holy Spirit he anointed his Son abundantly with the oil of gladness, that the heritage of human nature might be restored to its original glory. May the Lord our God most mighty, for the perfect blending of this oil and balm, grant the fullness of the + blessing of the Holy Trinity, and with that blessing + sanctify these substances. May the one who is anointed with this mixture of

COLLECTS AND READINGS

oil and balm receive the unction of the spirit, to be renewed in life, and fitted to enter into the light of the celestial kingdom. Through the same Lord Jesus Christ, in the unity of the same Holy Spirit, one God, throughout all ages.
R. Amen.

The bishop breathes once, in the form of a cross, over the Oil of Chrism. Simultaneously, the priests, remaining in their places, breathe once towards the Chrism. The bishop then says:

Creature of oil, I exorcize you in the name of God, the Father most mighty, who made the heavens and the earth, the seas, and all things contained within them, that you may be free from all powers of darkness and malice. Let those who are anointed with you, bear you as an ensign of their adoption as children of God through the Holy Spirit. In the name of God the almighty + Father, and of his Son Jesus Christ + our Lord, who lives and reigns with him in the unity of the same + Holy Spirit, one God, throughout all ages.
R. Amen.

The Chrism then receives its hallowing:

The Lord be with you.
R. And with your spirit.

Let us pray.

Holy and eternal God, when your Son, our Lord Jesus Christ, went to John for baptism in the waters of the Jordan, the Holy Spirit descended in the form of a dove, and your voice was heard in witness that Jesus was your beloved Son, in whom

COME AND WORSHIP

you were well pleased; and here was made manifest that which David had prophesied, when he spoke of the one who would be anointed with the oil of gladness. We therefore pray you, O Lord, holy Father, most mighty and ever-living God, that you + sanctify this precious creature with + your blessing, and with the + virtue of your Holy Spirit. May Christ lend his own power to this blessing, he from whose most holy name this oil is known as Chrism, this oil with which you have anointed priests and kings, prophets and martyrs. May this holy oil be a saving Chrism to those who are born again of water and the Holy Spirit, that they may inherit eternal life and share in heavenly glory. Through the same Jesus Christ, your Son, our Lord, who lives and reigns with you in the unity of the same Holy Spirit, one God, throughout all ages.
R. Amen.

The blessing of Oil of Catechumens now takes place.

The bishop breathes once in the form of a cross over the Oil of Catechumens; the priests, remaining in their places, likewise breathe once towards the oil. The bishop then exorcizes the oil:

Creature of oil, I exorcize you in the name of the Father + most mighty, and in the name of Jesus + Christ, and in the name of the Holy + Spirit; and in this invocation of the virtue of the undivided Trinity, of the power of the one and only godhead, I command all baleful influences, all confusion, all relentless hate, all phantasms and deceits of the adversary, to depart from you. Purified by this divine rite, be you fitted to adopt, body and soul, all who shall be anointed with you, for the

COLLECTS AND READINGS

remission of all sin; that they may be sanctified with every spiritual grace. Through the same Jesus Christ our Lord.
R. Amen.

The oil now receives its hallowing:

The Lord be with you.
R. And with your spirit.

Let us pray.

O God, your delight is in all that is conducive to spiritual advancement; and with the power of your Holy Spirit you strengthen our souls. Be pleased, O Lord, to + send forth your blessing upon this oil; and grant to those who approach the blessed regeneration of the waters of baptism a purification of soul and body by the anointing herewith. Let no influences of darkness remain with those who are anointed with this oil. When your children come to the Faith, and are ready for cleansing by the operation of the Holy Spirit, let this oil assist them in the salutary attainment of the celestial regeneration which is brought to birth in the Sacrament of Baptism. Through our Lord Jesus Christ.
R. Amen.

The clergy return to their places, the bishop goes to the altar, and the Mass is continued. Following the blessing at the end of the Mass, the sacred oils are borne to the sacristy by the appointed ministers.

Evening Mass of the Institution

The Introit of the Mass is said or sung:

COME AND WORSHIP

We should glory in the cross of our Lord Jesus Christ, for in him is our hope, our life and our resurrection; through him we are saved and made free.
May God pour forth his love upon us and bless us; may his face shine upon us and may his love enfold us.
Glory be to the Father, and to the Son, and to the Holy Spirit. As it was in the beginning, is now, and ever shall be, world without end. Amen.
We should glory in the cross of our Lord Jesus Christ, for in him is our hope, our life and our resurrection; through him we are saved and made free.

The Collect of the Mass:

Most mighty and eternal God, because of your so great love for all people, you sent your only Son, our Saviour Jesus Christ, to be born in this world, and to suffer death upon the cross, that we might follow the example of his great humility. Of your loving-kindness grant, we pray you, that we may both imitate his humility and have part in his resurrection. Through the same Jesus Christ our Lord, who lives and reigns with you and the Holy Spirit, one God, throughout all ages.
R. Amen.

Epistle: 1 Corinthians 11: 17-32
Gospel: John 13: 1-15

The blessing at the end of Mass is omitted. A veiled ciborium containing consecrated hosts is carried in procession to its place of repose, ready for Communion of the Reserved Sacrament on Good Friday. Aquinas' hymn, 'Pange, lingua, gloriosi, corporis mysterium', is

219

COLLECTS AND READINGS

sung as the procession begins:

Sing, my tongue, the Saviour's glory,
Of his flesh the mystery sing:
Lift on high the wondrous trophy,
Tell the triumph of the King:
He, the world's Redeemer, conquers
Death, through death now vanquishing.

Born for us, and for us given,
Born as human here below,
He, as man with us abiding,
Dwelt, the seeds of truth to sow;
And at last faced death undaunted,
Thus his greatest deed to show.

On the night of that last supper
Seated with his chosen band,
He, the paschal victim eating,
First fulfils the law's command,
Then as food to all his brethren,
Gives himself with his own hand.

Word made flesh! His word life-giving,
Gives his flesh our meat to be;
Bids us drink his blood, believing,
Through his death, we life shall see:
Blessed they who thus receiving
Are from death and sin set free.

Low in adoration bending,
Now our hearts our God revere;
Faith her aid to sight is lending,
Though unseen the Lord is near.
Ancient types and shadows ending,
Christ our paschal Lamb is here.

COME AND WORSHIP

Praise for ever, thanks and blessing,
Thine, O gracious Father, be;
Praise be thine, O Christ, who bringest
Life and immortality:
Praise be thine, thou quickening Spirit,
Praise through all eternity.

Amen.

Tr. Edward Caswall, 1814-78, and others.

Those who so desire may now, or at some time before midnight, dwell quietly in the presence of the reserved sacrament: so to keep watch with Christ 'for one hour' in the Garden of Gethsemane. But this time of reflection should not be continued beyond midnight.

Good Friday

Christ's Passion and Death

Black vestments are worn initially. No candles are lighted in church on this day. Mass is conducted as far as the conclusion of the Liturgy of the Word.

O God, by the passion of your Christ you have abolished death, the affliction of generations by cause of primal sin: grant us, we pray you, that we may become like unto Christ, that we who have of necessity borne the image of terrestrial nature may be sanctified with the seal of celestial grace. Through the same Christ our Lord, who lives and reigns with you and the Holy Spirit, one God, throughout all ages.

Epistle: Hebrews 10: 1-25

Now is said:

COLLECTS AND READINGS

The Passion of our Lord Jesus Christ, according to John.

The reading for the Passion is:

John 18: 1-40, 19: 1-37

Following the reading of the Passion, the Gospel is read:

Gospel: John 19: 38-42

At the conclusion of the Gospel, which here ends the Liturgy of the Word, the black vestments are removed, and the service proceeds as follows:

The Veneration of the Cross

A cross of wood (specifically, not a crucifix) is elevated by the celebrant, who says:

Behold the wood of the cross, where hung the Saviour of the world.
R. O come, let us adore.

The cross is placed before the altar by two ministers.

The celebrant first venerates it, genuflecting and kissing the lower part of the descending arm. He is followed by clergy and ministers, who venerate the cross in like fashion.

The cross is then placed conveniently for veneration by the faithful, and meanwhile the following is said or sung:

We adore your cross, O Lord, we praise and glorify

COME AND WORSHIP

your holy resurrection. For behold, by the wood of the cross the whole world was filled with rejoicing.
May God pour forth his love upon us and bless us; may the light of his face shine upon us, and may his love enfold us.
We adore your cross, O Lord, we praise and glorify your holy resurrection. For behold, by the wood of the cross the whole world was filled with joy.

The following hymn, the 'Pange, lingua, gloriosi, proelium certaminis' of Fortunatus, is now sung.

Sing, my tongue, the glorious battle,
sing the last, the dread affray;
o'er the cross, the victor's trophy,
sound the high triumphal lay,
how, the pains of death enduring,
earth's Redeemer won the day.

When at length th'appointed fullness
of the sacred time was come,
he was sent, the world's Creator,
from the Father's heavenly home,
and was found in human fashion,
offspring of the virgin's womb.

Now the thirty years are ended
which on earth he willed to see,
willingly he meets his passion,
born to set his people free;
on the cross the Lamb is lifted,
there the sacrifice to be.

There the nails and spear He suffers,
vinegar and gall and reed;

COLLECTS AND READINGS

from His sacred body piercèd
blood and water both proceed:
precious flood, which all creation
from the stain of sin hath freed.

Faithful Cross, above all other,
one and only noble Tree,
none in foliage, none in blossom,
none in fruit thy peer may be;
sweet the wood, and sweet the iron,
and thy load, most sweet is he.

Bend, O lofty Tree, thy branches,
thy too rigid sinews bend;
and awhile the stubborn hardness,
which thy birth bestowed, suspend;
and the limbs of heaven's high Monarch
gently on thine arms extend.

Thou alone wast counted worthy
this world's Ransom to sustain,
that a shipwrecked race for ever
might a port of refuge gain,
with the sacred Blood anointed
of the Lamb for sinners slain.

Praise and honour to the Father,
praise and honour to the Son,
praise and honour to the Spirit,
ever Three and ever One:
one in might, and One in glory,
while eternal ages run.

Tr. John Mason Neale, 1818-1866.

COME AND WORSHIP

The Communion Service

Following the veneration, the wooden cross is given a place of honour upon the altar.

The ministers now assume violet vestments. A corporal is spread on the altar, and the ciborium is brought from its place of repose and placed upon the altar by the celebrant or by the deacon.

First Antiphon:

We adore you, O Christ, and we bless you, for by your cross you have redeemed the world.

Second Antiphon:

By a tree we were made servants, and by the holy cross we are made free. The fruit of the tree seduced us; the Son of God redeems us.

Third Antiphon:

O Saviour of the world, save us! By your cross and your blood redeem us. O God, hear us, we pray you, and grant us your aid.

The Lord's Prayer:

Let us pray. In obedience to the command of our blessed Lord, and following the universal practice of his holy Church, let us say together:

Our Father who art in heaven, hallowed be thy name; thy kingdom come, thy will be done on earth as it is in heaven. Give us this day our daily bread; and forgive us our trespasses, as we

COLLECTS AND READINGS

forgive those who trespass against us. And lead us not into temptation, but deliver us from evil. Amen.

Prayer before Communion

Almighty God, our heavenly Father, we worship you in this hour with great tenderness of heart and purity of mind. Grant us, we pray you, that we may worthily receive the most precious body of your Son Jesus Christ, and be fulfilled with every grace and heavenly benediction and made one with him.
R. Amen.

Invitation to Communion

The priest then elevates a consecrated wafer above the ciborium, saying:

Behold the Lamb of God; behold him who takes away the sins of the world.

And all say:

Lord, I am not worthy to receive you, but only say the word and my soul shall be healed.

Communion

The priest receives a consecrated wafer:

May the body of our Lord Jesus Christ preserve my soul in everlasting life. Amen.

Clergy and servers receive, and then the faithful.

COME AND WORSHIP

May the body of our Lord Jesus Christ preserve
your soul in everlasting life.
R. Amen.

Final Prayer

All-powerful and loving God, by the blessed
passion and death of your Christ you have
renewed us. Grant us always to walk in the ways
of your loving kindness, and to participate with
fullness of heart, soul and mind in your holy
mysteries, that we may be filled with your grace
and ever devotedly live in you and for you.
Through the same Christ our Lord.
R. Amen.

Holy Saturday

Blessing of the New Fire

*Initially, the altar candles remain unlighted, and violet
vestments are worn.*
At the entrance to the temple the fire is blessed.

The Lord be with you.
R. And with your spirit.

O God, by that corner-stone which is your Son,
you have brought your children to the fire of your
glory: sanctify + this earthly fire, we pray you;
and grant that we may, through this Paschal
Feast, be so inflamed with celestial aspirations,
that we may come with pure minds and hearts to
the feast of your perpetual light. Through the
same Christ our Lord.
R. Amen.

COLLECTS AND READINGS

The fire is sprinkled with holy water, and then censed.

The Blessing of the Paschal Candle

The candle is brought by a minister to the celebrant, and is held before him.

The celebrant makes the sign of the cross before the candle, saying:

Christ, Yesterday and Today.
Beginning and End.
Alpha and Omega.
Time and the Ages belong to him.
To him be Glory and Power
For ever and ever. Amen.

The celebrant is given a taper, lighted from the new fire, whereupon he lights the candle, saying:

The light of Christ rises in glory, banishing the darkness of heart and of mind.

The Lord be with you.
R. And with your spirit.

Let your abundant blessing + come down upon this burning candle, we pray you, most mighty God. O you, the invisible giver of regeneration, graciously look upon this nocturnal splendour; may this night's sacrifice shine with the arcane refulgence of your own light. Wherever any least gleaming of this sacred fire is carried, there let your power dwell, to banish malice and darkness Through Christ our Lord, who lives and reigns with you and the Holy Spirit, one God, throughout all ages.
R. Amen.

COME AND WORSHIP

Procession and Exsultet

Incense is blessed and put into the thurible. The deacon, vested in white, receives the candle. In the procession, the thurifer is first, followed by a minister with the cross, the deacon, the celebrant, other clergy and ministers according to rank, and the faithful, all with unlighted candles.

The procession enters. The deacon halts, and then raises the paschal candle, chanting:

The Light of Christ.
R. Thanks be to God.

The celebrant lights his own candle from the paschal candle, and the procession resumes. At the middle of the church the deacon halts, raises the paschal candle, and in a higher tone chants:

The Light of Christ.
R. Thanks be to God.

The other clergy, and the ministers, light their candles from the paschal candle, and the procession resumes. When the procession reaches the altar, the deacon halts, turns to face the people, raises the paschal candle, and chants in a higher key:

The Light of Christ.
R. Thanks be to God.

The people now light their candles from the paschal candle. Where expedient, the light may be transmitted from the candle of one person to that of another.

The church is then illuminated, but the altar candles remain unlit.

COLLECTS AND READINGS

Incense is blessed by the priest and put into the thurible, which is held by a minister.

The deacon sets the paschal candle in its place in the sanctuary, and then goes to the priest, and kneels before the priest says:

On this night, I pray that I may proclaim the Easter praise with joy and purity of mind.

The priest blesses the deacon:

May the Lord be in your heart and on your lips, that you may well and worthily proclaim the Easter praise. In the name of the Father, and of the + Son, and of the Holy Spirit. Amen.

Exsultet

The deacon arises and goes to the lectern, accompanied by two ministers, who bear the book containing the Exsultet and the thurible. The deacon receives the book and places it upon the lectern. He receives the thurible and censes the book, and then goes to the paschal candle, censing it five times. The thurible is then returned to the minister, who holds it while the deacon chants or says the Exsultet at the lectern.

Let the angelic choirs of heaven rejoice, let the unseen beings that dwell with God rejoice. Let the trumpet of salvation be sounded to proclaim the victory of the king. Joyful be the earth in the radiance of this glory; shining in the splendour of her king, let her rejoice that darkness has been lifted from all the world. Let mother Church rejoice, robed in the brilliance of a light so

COME AND WORSHIP

wonderful. Let these walls resound joyfully as they echo the acclamations of the people.

Christians, you who stand with me in the beauty of this light, join with me in invocation of the great and loving kindness of God most mighty: may he pour forth his glory upon me, his undeserving minister, that I may be enabled to dignify this candle with worthy and perfect praise. Through Jesus Christ his Son our Lord, who lives and reigns with him in the unity of the Holy Spirit, one God, throughout all ages.
R. Amen.

The Lord be with you.
R. And with your spirit.

Lift up your hearts.
R. We lift them to the Lord.

Let us give thanks to the Lord our God.
R. It is right to give him thanks and praise

It is truly right and our greatest joy to give you thanks and praise, with all the power of heart and mind to proclaim your praises, O invisible God, Father most mighty, and the praises of Jesus Christ your only Son. For it was Christ who repaid Adam's debt to you, and who with his precious blood erased our ancient bondage. The paschal feast is here, and the true Lamb is slain: the Lamb whose very blood sanctifies the doorposts of your children.

On this night, O Lord, you brought our ancestors out of Egypt, and led them through the waters of

COLLECTS AND READINGS

the Red Sea.

On this night, the light of the fiery pillar drove away the darkness of failure.

On this night, we are restored in grace and united in holiness.

On this night, Christ broke the bonds of death, and rose victorious from the tomb.

How wondrous and beyond all comprehension is the love you have shown to us.

To liberate us, you gave your Son.

Needful the fault of Adam's sin, for the death of Christ was its atonement.

Needful the fault, warranting such a redeemer.

Truly blessed is this night, no other night so blessed: night that proclaims Christ's triumph over death.

This is the night of which scripture says: The night shall shine as the day!

On this holy night, evil is dispelled, sin is cleansed, innocence is restored, joy is brought to those who mourn, hatreds cease, harmony dwells among us, and pride is humbled.

In this night's grace, O holy God, receive the incense of this evening sacrifice, this solemn offering of flame, this candle formed of wax from

COME AND WORSHIP

the bee.

A brilliant fire burns here in honour of God: a fire that has divided into many flames, yet has retained its original splendour.

We pray you, Lord: may this candle, sanctified in honour of your name, burn unfailingly to dispel the darkness of this night. Accept it as a fragrant incense, and let its radiance mingle with that of the celestial lights.

May the morning star find its flame still burning, that star which sets not, which arose from death to enlighten all humanity.

The candles of the people are extinguished. The deacon removes the white vestments and puts on violet vestments. The lesson is read by a lector.

First Lesson

Genesis 1: 1-31, 2: 1-2

These verses are sung after the first lesson:

Rejoice in the Lord, O you righteous: for praise is comely for the upright.
For the word of the Lord is right: and all his works are accomplished in truth.
The Lord loves righteousness and truth: the earth is filled with the goodness of the Lord.
By the word of the Lord the heavens were made: and all the hosts of heaven by the breath of his mouth.
The Lord gathers the waters together: the Lord

COLLECTS AND READINGS

lays the deeps as in treasure chambers.
Let the whole earth reverence the Lord: let all peoples of the world stand in awe of him.
The Lord spoke, and it was done: the Lord commanded, and it was established.

The celebrant says:

Let us pray.

O God, you wonderfully fashioned us, and yet more wonderfully redeemed us: grant us, we pray, that by walking always in the path of your commandments we may be found worthy to enter into eternal bliss. Through Jesus Christ our Lord, who lives and reigns with you and the Holy Spirit, one God, throughout all ages.
R. Amen.

A lector reads the second lesson:

Second Lesson

Genesis 22: 1-18

After the second lesson, these verses are sung:

The Lord is the portion of my inheritance and my cup.
I have set the Lord always before me; because he is near to me I shall not be moved.
Therefore my heart is glad and my glory rejoices.
He will show me the path of life: in his presence is fullness of joy, at his right hand are pleasures for evermore.

The priest says:

COME AND WORSHIP

Let us pray.

O God, you promised to Abraham that he would be the parent of nations, in multitudes as the stars of heaven. In Christ is that promise fulfilled: for through his death and resurrection you increase your chosen people in all the earth. May we hear and answer the voice of your calling, as you invite us to the life of grace which is the regeneration. Through the same Christ our Lord, who lives and reigns with you and the Holy Spirit, one God, throughout all ages.
R. Amen.

Third Lesson

Exodus 14: 24-31, 15: 1

This canticle is now sung:

Then Moses and the children of Israel sang this song to the Lord, saying: I will praise the Lord, the mighty, the glorious. Horse and rider he has hurled into the sea.
The Lord is my strength and my song: he is my salvation, he is my God. I will prepare him a dwelling place.

The priest says:

Let us pray.

O God, even now, in our own day, we see your ancient wonders: for even as the right hand of your power gave salvation to one people, freeing them from Egyptian bondage, so now your

COLLECTS AND READINGS

salvation extends to all peoples by means of the waters of regeneration. Through our Lord Jesus Christ, who lives and reigns with you and the Holy Spirit, one God, throughout all ages.
R. Amen.

A lector reads the fourth lesson:

Fourth Lesson

Isaiah 4: 2-6

This canticle is sung:

Now will I sing to my well-beloved: a song of my beloved touching his vineyard.
My beloved has a vineyard in a very fruitful hill: and he fenced it, and gathered out the stones thereof, and planted it with a vine of Sorec.
And he built a tower in the midst of it: and he also established a winepress therein.
This vineyard of the Lord of Hosts: it is the house of Israel!

The priest says:

O God, your prophets have declared it: everywhere, in your glorious kingdom and in your elect children, you plant fertile seed, and bring to fullness of growth the tender vine. Grant, O most mighty, that we, your seedlings, planted in the vineyard which is your holy Church, may always abundantly flourish in the beauty of holiness, to the honour of your name. Through Jesus Christ our Lord.

COME AND WORSHIP

Fifth Lesson

Isaiah 55: 1-11

These verses are sung:

And in that day you shall say, O Lord, I will praise you: though you were angry with me, your anger is turned away and you comfort me.
Behold, God is my salvation, I will trust and not be afraid: for the Lord Jehovah is my strength and my song, and he is become my salvation.
Joyfully, then, shall you draw water: even from the wells of salvation.
And in that day you shall say, Praise the Lord, invoke his name: make known his deeds among the people, proclaim that his name is exalted.
Sing to the Lord, for he has done excellent things: this is known in all the earth.
Cry aloud, O you who dwell in Zion: for great is the holy One of Israel in the midst of you.

The priest now says:

Let us pray.

O Lord our God, most mighty, eternal: the divine mysteries of our worship this night were proclaimed by the voice of your prophets. O you, the inspiration of our hearts and minds, grant that we may ever grow in holiness in the light of your word. Through Jesus Christ our Lord, who lives and reigns with you and the Holy Spirit, one God, throughout all ages.
R. Amen.

COLLECTS AND READINGS

If baptismal water is not be prepared during this rite, the following section, Blessing of Baptismal Water, *is omitted, and the priest changes violet vestments for white stole and cope. The deacon also vests in white, and priest and ministers go in silence to the sanctuary for the* Renewal of Baptismal Promises. *In this case ordinary Holy Water is used for the aspersion.*

If baptismal water is to be blessed, then the violet vestments are retained, the rite proceeding as follows:

Blessing of Baptismal Water

A vessel for the water, a ewer of pure water, and a phial of blessed salt are made ready, upon a small table, before the altar, near the paschal candle. Facing the people across the vessel, the priest says:

The Lord be with you
R. And with your spirit.

Let us pray.

Eternal and most mighty God, be with us, and ratify these holy mysteries of your love towards us. Send forth the Spirit of adoption, that all who are born to you from the waters of baptism may be recreated in newness of life. Through Jesus Christ our Lord, who lives and reigns with you in the unity of the Holy Spirit, one God, throughout all ages.
R. Amen.

The priest pours water from the ewer into the vessel.

It is truly right and our greatest joy to give you thanks and praise, eternal and living God, Lord

COME AND WORSHIP

most mighty, by whose hidden power the sacraments have wonderful effect. In the beginning your Spirit moved upon the face of the deep, even then endowing the element of water with the power to sanctify. By the waters of the flood you cleansed the world of its failings; and sealed the symbol of regeneration. Thus this one same element became, in mystery, the ending of weakness and the origin of virtue. In your kindness, O Lord, look upon the face of your Church, and increase her offspring, the regenerated; for you are the same God who makes glad your city with the outpoured abundance of grace, and who opens the fountain of baptism to all people, that they may receive the grace of the only-begotten from the Holy Spirit.

Using the right hand, the priest makes the sign of the cross in horizontal plane above the surface of the water (west-east, south-north).

Let this very water, then, be prepared for the regeneration of the sons and daughters of God: let it be freed from all adverse and inimical conditions, and let it be made fruitful by the arcane infusion of divine power.

The priest puts salt, which has previously been exorcised and blessed, crosswise into the water. Then, touching the water, the priest says:

May this holy and innocent creature be free of the assaults of the enemy, and purged by the withdrawal of every kind of iniquity. Let it be a fount of life, a water of regeneration: that all who shall know its salvific touch may, by the operation of the Holy Spirit, be perfectly purified.

COLLECTS AND READINGS

The priest now signs the cross thrice over the water:

Wherefore I bless you, creature of water, by the living + God, by the true + God, by the holy + God, by God whose word in the beginning separated you from the dry land, whose Spirit moved upon you.

Who bade you to flow forth from a spring in Eden, to water the garden, and thence to divide into four streams to water the whole earth.

Who transformed your bitterness to sweetness in the wilderness, and caused you to gush forth from a rock that you might quench the people's thirst.

He signs the cross over the water, as indicated:

I bless you, too, + through God's only Son Jesus Christ, our Lord, who at Cana in Galilee miraculously changed you into wine, who walked upon you, who was baptised in you by John in the Jordan, and who commanded his disciples to baptise believers in you, saying, Go, instruct the nations, baptising them in the name of the Father, and of the Son, and of the Holy Spirit.

Most mighty God, be with us + in your great and loving kindness, and breathe forth your goodness upon us.

The priest breathes thrice upon the face of the water, crosswise, and says:

Let the power of the Holy Spirit descend into the fullness of this vessel.

COME AND WORSHIP

The priest signs the water with the cross, as indicated:

Wholly to imbue + the substance of this water with the fruitful power to regenerate: that human nature may here be restored to its primal innocence and to the splendour of its divine original through the sacrament of regeneration. Through Jesus Christ your Son, our Lord.
R. Amen.

Some blessed water is now reserved for use as holy water, during the renewal of baptismal promises following, and for other intended purposes.

The priest now removes the violet vestments and assumes a white stole. If there are baptisms, they are conducted in the usual manner, but beginning from the Apostles' Creed and before the blessed water is carried to the font.

The vessel of baptismal water is carried to the font, while the following hymn is sung:

As pants the hart for cooling streams
When heated in the chase,
So longs my soul, O God, for thee,
And thy refreshing grace.

For thee, my God, the living God,
My thirsty soul doth pine,
O when shall I behold thy face,
Thou majesty divine?

God of my strength, how long shall I,
Like one forsaken, mourn:
Forlorn, forsaken, and exposed
To my oppressor's scorn?

COLLECTS AND READINGS

Why restless, why cast down, my soul?
Hope still, and thou shalt sing
The praise of him who is thy God,
Thy health's eternal spring.

To Father, Son and Holy Ghost,
The God whom we adore,
Be glory, as it was, is now,
And shall be evermore.

Nahum Tate 1659-1715, and
Nicholas Brady 1659-1726.

The celebrant assumes a white cope. The baptismal water is poured into the font.

The Lord be with you.
R. And with your spirit.

Let us pray.

Ever-living and all-potent God, graciously look upon your devoted people. As the hart longs for cooling streams, so do they yearn for your waters. Grant that their thirst for faith may, through the baptismal mystery, sanctify them in body and soul. Through our Lord Jesus Christ, your Son, who lives and reigns with you in the unity of the Holy Spirit, one God, throughout all ages.
R. Amen.

The celebrant blesses incense, and the font is censed. Then clergy and ministers process in silence to the sanctuary

COME AND WORSHIP

Renewal of Baptismal Promises

All standing, the celebrant censes the paschal candle five times, resigns the thurible, and then says:

Christians, in this most sacred night our holy mother the Church keeps vigil, mindful of the death and burial of the Lord Jesus Christ; and she celebrates the glorious resurrection of Christ with joyful praise.

In baptism we mystically die and are buried in Christ; but even as Christ conquered death, so must we too enter into the glorious regeneration, taking hold of the New Life. Our former self has been crucified with Christ, that the ancient bondage of sin may be annulled; but now we are no more in bondage to sin: we are alive to God, in our Lord Jesus Christ.

Christians, now that we have reached this place of faith and hope and aspiration, let us renew the promises made at our baptism: to renounce Satan and the works of darkness, and to love God and the works of light.

I ask, therefore:

Do you renounce Satan?
R. We renounce him.

Do you renounce all his works?
R. We renounce them.

Do you renounce all his vain glories and deceits?
R. We renounce them.

COLLECTS AND READINGS

Do you believe in God, the all-potent and eternal creator of heaven and earth?
R. We do believe.

Do you believe in Jesus Christ, God's only Son our Lord, who was incarnate in this world and who suffered for us?
R. We do believe.

Do you believe in the Holy Spirit, the holy catholic Church, the communion of saints, the forgiveness of sins, the resurrection of the body and the life everlasting?
R. We do believe.

Let us pray. In obedience to the command of our blessed Lord, let us say:

Our Father who art in heaven, hallowed be thy name; thy kingdom come, thy will be done on earth as it is in heaven. Give us this day our daily bread; and forgive us our trespasses, as we forgive those who trespass against us. And lead us not into temptation, but deliver us from evil. Amen.

May the most mighty God, the Father of our Lord Jesus Christ, who has regenerated us with water and the Holy Spirit, and granted us remission of our sins, keep us by his grace in the same Lord Jesus Christ, in life eternal.
R. Amen.

The celebrant sprinkles the people with the holy water that was earlier reserved (or with the usual holy water, if baptismal water was not blessed).

COME AND WORSHIP

*The altar candles are lighted, while the clergy vest for
the Eucharistic Liturgy.*

Mass of the Easter Vigil

*The preparatory prayers are omitted, and the Liturgy
commences with the Kyrie eleison.*

*While this is being sung the priest and the ministers,
vested in white, go to the altar.*

The celebrant kisses the altar, which is then censed.

The Gloria in excelsis is sung.

The Collect of the Mass is said:

O God, you illumine this most sacred night with
the glory of our Lord's resurrection: preserve in
the children of your new household the spirit of
adoption you have bestowed upon them, so that,
being renewed in body and soul, they may show
forth purity and innocence in your service.
Through the same Jesus Christ our Lord, who lives
and reigns with you in the unity of the Holy Spirit,
one God, throughout all ages.

The Epistle is read.

Epistle: Colossians 3: 1-4

Acclamation

This text is said or sung by all:

**Alleluia! Alleluia! Alleluia!
O Praise the Lord, all you nations: praise him,**

COLLECTS AND READINGS

all you peoples.
For his great loving kindness: is ever more and more towards us;
And the truth of the Lord endures for ever: praise the Lord.

Following the Munda cor meum, the Gospel is read.

Lights are not here carried at the Gospel reading.

Gospel: Matthew 28: 1-7

The Affirmation of Faith is omitted, as is the opening Offertory text. The Preface of Easter is used. In the Rite of Communion, the Peace is omitted; and if Agnus Dei forms part of the rite, this too is omitted.

The rite proceeds as usual to the Ablutions, but is thereafter concluded with a contracted form of the Office of Lauds, as follows.

Psalm 150 is sung:

Alleluia! Alleluia! Alleluia!

O praise God in his holiness: praise him in the firmament of his power.
Praise him in his noble acts: praise him according to his excellent greatness.
Praise him in the sound of the trumpet: praise him upon the lute and harp.
Praise him in the cymbals and dances: praise him upon the strings and pipe.
Praise him upon the well-tuned cymbals: praise him upon the loud cymbals.
Let everything that has breath: praise the Lord!
Glory be to the Father, and to the Son: and to the

COME AND WORSHIP

Holy Spirit. As it was in the beginning, is now, and ever shall be: world without end. Amen.

Alleluia! Alleluia! Alleluia!

The following antiphon is chanted by the celebrant alone, who then censes the altar while the Benedictus is sung.

On the dawn of the following Sabbath they came to the tomb, and the sun had already risen. Alleluia!

Benedictus

Blessed be the Lord God of Israel: for he hath visited and redeemed his people;
And hath raised up a mighty salvation for us: in the house of his servant David;
As he spake by the mouth of his holy prophets: which have been since the world began;
That we should be saved from our enemies: and from the hands of all that hate us;
To perform the mercy promised to our forefathers: and to remember his holy covenant;
To perform the oath which he sware to our forefather Abraham, that he would give us: that we, being delivered out of the hand of our enemies, might serve him without fear, in holiness and righteousness before him, all the days of our life.
And thou, Child, shall be called the prophet of the most high: for thou shalt go before the face of the Lord to prepare his way;
To give knowledge of salvation unto his people, for the remission of their sins, through the tender

COLLECTS AND READINGS

mercy of our God: whereby the dayspring from on high hath visited us;
To give light to them that sit in darkness, and in the shadow of death: and to guide our feet into the way of peace.
Gory be to the Father, and to the Son: and to the Holy Spirit.
As it was in the beginning, is now, and ever shall be: world without end. Amen.

The celebrant again sings the antiphon.

On the dawn of the following Sabbath they came to the tomb, and the sun had already risen. Alleluia!

The Lord be with you.
R. And with your spirit.

Let us pray.

Infuse our spirit with your love, O Lord, that we who have been nourished with this paschal sacrament may, of your great and loving kindness, be of one accord. Through Jesus Christ your Son, our Lord, who lives and reigns with you and the Holy Spirit, one God, throughout all ages.
R. Amen.

The dismissal is made by celebrant or deacon.

The Mass is ended. Go forth in the Light of Christ.
The celebrant gives the blessing:

May almighty God bless you: the Father, the + Son, and the Holy Spirit.
R. Amen.

COME AND WORSHIP

EASTER

Feast of the Resurrection

O God, through your only-begotten Son you have this day triumphed over death and opened to us the gate of life eternal: assist us, we pray you, to fulfill the longings which you yourself first breathed into us. Through the same Jesus Christ your Son, our Lord, who lives and reigns with you and the Holy Spirit, one God, throughout all ages.

Epistle: 1 Corinthians 5: 7-8

Gospel Acclamation

This is the day that the Lord has made: we will be glad and rejoice in it.
Give thanks to the Lord for he is good: his love endures for ever.

The Alleluia

Alleluia! Alleluia!
Christ our Passover has been sacrificed for us.

Sequence

Christians, to the Paschal victim
offer your thankful praises!
A lamb the sheep redeemeth:
Christ, who only is sinless,
reconcileth sinners to the Father.
Death and life have contended
in that combat stupendous:
the Prince of life, who died,

COLLECTS AND READINGS

reigns immortal.
Speak, Mary, declaring
what thou sawest, wayfaring:
"The tomb of Christ, who is living,
the glory of Jesus' resurrection;
Bright angels attesting,
the shroud and napkin resting.
Yea, Christ my hope is arisen;
to Galilee he will go before you".
Christ indeed from death is risen,
our new life obtaining;
have mercy, victor King, ever reigning!
Amen.

Tr. Antiphoner and Grail, 1880.

Gospel: Mark 16: 1-7

Monday in Easter Week

O God, through your only-begotten Son you have triumphed over death and opened to us the gate of life eternal: assist us, we pray you, to fulfil the longings which you yourself first breathed into us. Through the same Jesus Christ your Son, our Lord, who lives and reigns with you and the Holy Spirit, one God, throughout all ages.

Epistle: Acts 10: 37-43
Gospel: Luke 24: 13-35

Tuesday in Easter Week

O God, through your only-begotten Son you have triumphed over death and opened to us the gate of life eternal: assist us, we pray you, to fulfil the longings which you yourself first breathed into us.

COME AND WORSHIP

Through the same Jesus Christ your Son, our Lord, who lives and reigns with you and the Holy Spirit, one God, throughout all ages.

Epistle: Acts 13: 16, 26-33
Gospel: Luke 24: 36-47

Wednesday in Easter Week

O God, through your only-begotten Son you have triumphed over death and opened to us the gate of life eternal: assist us, we pray you, to fulfil the longings which you yourself first breathed into us. Through the same Jesus Christ your Son, our Lord, who lives and reigns with you and the Holy Spirit, one God, throughout all ages.

Epistle: Acts 3: 13-15, 17-19
Gospel: John 21: 1-14

Thursday in Easter Week

O God, in the confession of your holy name you have made diversity of nations one family: may the new birth of the baptismal font bring us unity in our faith and cause us to be pious in our actions. Through Jesus Christ your Son, our Lord, who lives and reigns with you and the Holy Spirit, one God, throughout all ages.

Epistle: Acts 8: 26-40
Gospel: John 20: 11-18

Friday in Easter Week

Most mighty and eternal God, you made a

COLLECTS AND READINGS

covenant of reconciliation with all people by the holy paschal mystery: grant us always to be true to this same covenant, we pray you. Through Jesus Christ your Son, our Lord, who lives and reigns with you and the Holy Spirit, one God, throughout all ages.

Epistle 1 Peter 3: 18-22
Gospel: Matthew 28: 16-20

Saturday in Easter Week

O God, through your only-begotten Son you have triumphed over death and opened to us the gate of life eternal: assist us, we pray you, to fulfil the longings which you yourself first breathed into us. Through the same Jesus Christ your Son, our Lord, who lives and reigns with you and the Holy Spirit, one God, throughout all ages.

Epistle: 1 Peter 2: 1-10
Gospel: John 20: 1-9

Second Sunday of Easter

All-potent God, you gave your only Son to die for us, and to rise again for our justification. Grant, we pray you, that we may put away from us the leaven of unworthiness, so that we may ever minister to you in purity of life and truth. Through the same Jesus Christ your Son, our Lord, who lives and reigns with you and the Holy Spirit, one God, throughout all ages.

Epistle: 1 John 5: 4-12
Gospel: John 20: 19-31

COME AND WORSHIP

Third Sunday of Easter

God of all power, you gave your only Son to be both the acceptable sacrifice and the example of honourable life. By your grace, most holy, grant that we may always receive the benefits of his love reverently and with heartfelt thanks, and also that we may follow daily in his blessed footsteps. Through the same Jesus Christ your Son, our Lord, who lives and reigns with you and the Holy Spirit, one God, throughout all ages.

Epistle: 1 Peter 2: 21-25
Gospel: John 10: 11-16

Fourth Sunday of Easter

O God, you show to wanderers the light of your truth, calling them to follow the way of righteousness: grant your aid, we pray you, to all who profess themselves Christian, that they may walk worthily, and with honour, in their pilgrimage. Through Jesus Christ your Son, our Lord, who lives and reigns with you and the Holy Spirit, one God, throughout all ages.

Epistle: 1 Peter 2: 11-19
Gospel: John 16: 16-22

Fifth Sunday of Easter

God of might eternal, graciously grant the minds of your people to be united in love of your precepts and in holy desire of the bliss you have promised, that their hearts may continually dwell in you, the true joy of all the worlds. Through

COLLECTS AND READINGS

Jesus Christ your Son, our Lord, who lives and reigns with you and the Holy Spirit, one God, throughout all ages.

Epistle: James 1: 17-21
Gospel: John 16: 5-14

Sixth Sunday of Easter

Lord of light and life, from whom all good things do proceed, grant to your people, by your holy inspiration, always to rise to the best and the noblest in thought and deed, and by your loving guidance to achieve the same. Through Jesus Christ your Son, our Lord, who lives and reigns with you and the Holy Spirit, one God, throughout all ages.

Epistle: James 1: 22-27
Gospel: John 16: 23-30

Holy Thursday (Feast of the Ascension)

All-powerful God, as we believe and profess that your only Son ascended into the celestial realms, so may we in hearts and minds ascend likewise, that our souls may continually dwell in the light of his presence. Through the same Jesus Christ your Son, our Lord, who lives and reigns with you and the Holy Spirit, one God, throughout all ages.

Epistle: Acts 1: 1-11
Gospel: Mark 16: 14-20

COME AND WORSHIP

Seventh Sunday of Easter

O God, most glorious and eternal: grant that we may always devotedly serve your divine majesty with sincerity of heart. Through Jesus Christ your Son our Lord, who lives and reigns with you and the Holy Spirit, one God, throughout all ages.

Epistle: 1 Peter 4: 7-11
Gospel: John 15: 26-27, 16: 1-4

PENTECOST

Pentecost Sunday

O God, who on this day taught the hearts of your people by the light of your Holy and Life-giving Spirit, grant that the Paraclete may guide us in rightness of thought and, comforting us, ever cause us to know joy in heart and soul. Through Jesus Christ your Son, our Lord, who lives and reigns with you and the same Holy Spirit, one God, throughout all ages.

Epistle: Acts 2: 1-11

Gospel Acclamation

Alleluia! Alleluia!
You send forth your Spirit, and they are created;
and you renew the face of the earth. Alleluia!
Come, Holy Spirit, fill the hearts of your faithful,
And kindle within them the fire of your love.

Following the Acclamation, and before the reading of the Gospel, the Golden Sequence is sung:

COLLECTS AND READINGS

The Golden Sequence

Come, thou Holy Spirit, come!
And from thy celestial home
Shed a ray of light divine!
Come, thou Father of the poor!
Come, thou source of all our store!
Come, within our bosoms shine!
Thou, of comforters the best;
Thou, the soul's most welcome guest;
Sweet refreshment here below;
In our labour, rest most sweet;
Grateful coolness in the heat;
Solace in the midst of woe.
O most blessèd light divine,
Shine within these hearts of thine,
And our inmost being fill!
Where thou art not, we have naught,
Nothing good in deed or thought,
Nothing free from taint of ill.
Heal our wounds, our strength renew;
On our dryness pour thy dew;
Wash the stains of guilt away;
Bend the stubborn heart and will;
Melt the frozen, warm the chill;
Guide the steps that go astray.
On the faithful, who adore
And confess thee, evermore
In thy sev'nfold gift descend;
Give them virtue's sure reward
Give them thy salvation, Lord;
Give them joys that never end.
Amen! Alleluia!

Tr. Edward Caswall, 1814-78.

Gospel: John 14: 23-31

COME AND WORSHIP

Monday after Pentecost

O God, who on this day taught the hearts of your people by the light of your Holy and Life-giving Spirit, grant that the Paraclete may guide us in rightness of thought and, comforting us, ever cause us to know joy in heart and soul. Through Jesus Christ your Son, our Lord, who lives and reigns with you and the same Holy Spirit, one God, throughout all ages.

Epistle: Acts 10: 34-38
Gospel: John 3: 16-21

Tuesday after Pentecost

O God, who on this day taught the hearts of your people by the light of your Holy and Life-giving Spirit, grant that the Paraclete may guide us in rightness of thought and, comforting us, ever cause us to know joy in heart and soul. Through Jesus Christ your Son, our Lord, who lives and reigns with you and the same Holy Spirit, one God, throughout all ages.

Epistle: Acts 8: 14-17
Gospel: John 10: 1-10

TRINITY

Trinity Sunday

Most potent, ever-living God, you have endowed your people with grace to confess the true faith, to proclaim the glory of the eternal Trinity, and in the power of the divine majesty to adore the

COLLECTS AND READINGS

unity. Keep us steadfast in this faith, that we may ever be defended from all adversities. Through Christ our Lord.

Epistle: Revelation 4: 1-11
Gospel: John 3: 1-15

Thursday after Trinity Sunday (Corpus Christi)

O God, you who in this wonderful sacrament have left us a memorial of your passion: grant us so to venerate the sacred mysteries of your body and blood that we may ever know within ourselves the fruits of your redemption; you who live and reign with God the Father in the unity of the Holy Spirit, one God, throughout all ages.

Epistle: 1 Corinthians 11: 23-29

Acclamation

Alleluia! Alleluia!
My flesh is true food,
And my blood is true drink.
Those who eat my flesh and drink my blood,
Live in me, and I in them.

Sequence

Laud, O Sion, thy salvation,
laud with hymns of exultation
Christ, thy King and Shepherd true.
Spend thyself, his honour raising,
who surpasseth all thy praising;
never canst thou reach his due.

COME AND WORSHIP

Sing today, the mystery showing
of the living, life bestowing
Bread from heaven before thee set;
e'en the same of old provided,
where the Twelve, divinely guided,
at the holy table met.

Full and clear ring out thy chanting,
joy nor sweetest grace be wanting
to thy heart and soul today;
when we gather up the measure
of that Supper and its treasure,
keeping feast in glad array.

Lo, the new King's table gracing,
this new Passover of blessing
hath fulfilled the elder rite;
now the new the old effaceth,
truth revealed the shadow chaseth,
day is breaking on the night.

What he did at Supper seated,
Christ ordained to be repeated,
his memorial ne'er to cease:
and, his word for guidance taking,
bread and wine we hallow, making
thus our sacrifice of peace.

This the truth to Christians given:
Bread becomes his Flesh from heaven,
Wine becomes his holy Blood.
Doth it pass thy comprehending?
Yet by faith, thy sight transcending,
wondrous things are understood.

COLLECTS AND READINGS

Yea, beneath these signs are hidden
glorious things to sight forbidden:
look not on the outward sign.
Wine is poured and Bread is broken,
but in either sacred token
Christ is here by power divine.

Whoso of this Food partaketh,
rendeth not the Lord nor breaketh:
Christ is whole to all that taste.
Thousands are, as one, receivers,
one, as thousands of believers,
takes the Food that cannot waste.

When the Sacrament is broken,
doubt not in each severed token,
hallowed by the word once spoken,
resteth all the true content:
nought the precious Gift divideth,
breaking but the sign betideth,
he himself the same abideth,
nothing of his fullness spent.

Lo! the Angel's Food is given
To the pilgrim who hath striven;
See the children's Bread from heaven,
Which to dogs may not be cast;
Truth the ancient types fulfilling;
Isaac bound, a victim willing;
Paschal lamb, its life-blood spilling;
Manna sent in ages past.

O true Bread, good Shepherd, tend us,
Jesu of thy love befriend us,
Thou refresh us, thou defend us,
Thine eternal goodness send us

COME AND WORSHIP

In the land of life to see;

Thou who all things canst and knowest,
Who on earth such Food bestowest,
Grant us with thy Saints though lowest,
Where the heavenly Feast thou shewest,
Fellow-heirs and guests to be.
Amen. Alleluia.

Tr. Composite, English Hymnal, 1906

Gospel: John 6: 56-59

SUNDAYS AFTER TRINITY

First Sunday after Trinity

O God, our strength, our rock in whom we trust, in your loving kindness receive the prayers of your people: for without you we are powerless, and can accomplish no deed of lasting worth. Aid us, then, with your grace, that in remaining faithful to your precepts we may please you, in will and in deed. Through Jesus Christ your Son, our Lord, who lives and reigns with you and the Holy Spirit, one God, throughout all ages.

Epistle: 1 John 4: 7-21
Gospel: Luke 16: 19-31

Second Sunday after Trinity

Your protection, Lord, is with us, your right arm defends us, for your regard is never-failing towards those who steadfastly honour your commands: grant us therefore, O Lord, we who are dwellers within the shadow of your wings, to

COLLECTS AND READINGS

manifest an unending reverence and love of your holy name. Through Jesus Christ your Son, our Lord, who lives and reigns with you and the Holy Spirit, one God, throughout all ages.

Epistle: 1 John 3: 13-24
Gospel: Luke 14: 16-24

Third Sunday after Trinity

In your great and loving kindness hear us, O Lord, and grant that we, to whom you have given a good desire to pray, may by your aid be defended and comforted in all danger and adversity. Through Christ our Lord.

Epistle: 1 Peter 5: 2-11
Gospel: Luke 15: 1-10

Fourth Sunday after Trinity

O God, protector of all who place their trust in you, without whom nothing is strong, nothing holy: pour forth upon us your love, and grant that we may so pass through this temporal world that at the last we may be found worthy of eternal life. Through Jesus Christ your Son, our Lord, who lives and reigns with you and the Holy Spirit, one God, throughout all ages.

Epistle: Romans 8: 18-23
Gospel: Luke 6: 36-45

Fifth Sunday after Trinity

O Lord, may the course of this world be so

COME AND WORSHIP

harmoniously governed by you, that your Church may joyfully serve you in holy peace. Through Jesus Christ your Son, our Lord, who lives and reigns with you and the Holy Spirit, one God, throughout all ages.

Epistle: 1 Peter 3: 8-15
Gospel: Luke 5: 1-11

Sixth Sunday after Trinity

O God, you have prepared for those that love you such good things as transcend our understanding: pour into our hearts a great love towards you, that, loving you above all things, we may obtain your promises, which exceed all that we can hope or desire. Through Jesus Christ your Son, our Lord, who lives and reigns with you and the Holy Spirit, one God, throughout all ages.

Epistle: Romans 6: 3-11
Gospel: Matthew 5: 20-26

Seventh Sunday after Trinity

Lord of power and might, author and giver of all good things: graft in our hearts the love of your holy name, increase in us true religion, and of your great and loving kindness keep us in the same. Through Jesus Christ your Son, our Lord, who lives and reigns with you and the Holy Spirit, one God, throughout all ages.

Epistle: Romans 6: 19-23
Gospel: Mark 8: 1-9

COLLECTS AND READINGS

Eighth Sunday after Trinity

O God, your providence orders all things, both celestial and terrestrial: grant us your aid, we pray you, that we may walk safely amid the perils of this world, and achieve those things that are profitable to the soul. Through Jesus Christ your Son, our Lord, who lives and reigns with you and the Holy Spirit, one God, throughout all ages.

Epistle: Romans 8: 12-17
Gospel: Matthew 7: 15-21

Ninth Sunday after Trinity

Gracious Lord, grant us the spirit to think and to perform the things which are rightful in your sight: that we may, by your divine help, be enabled to live in accordance with your will. Through Jesus Christ your Son, our Lord, who lives and reigns with you and the Holy Spirit, one God, throughout all ages.

Epistle: 1 Corinthians 10: 1-13
Gospel: Luke 15: 1-32

Tenth Sunday after Trinity

In your great kindness, O Lord, hear the prayers of your people: and that they may obtain their petitions, cause them to ask, in spiritual harmony with you, such things as shall please you. Through Jesus Christ your Son, our Lord, who lives and reigns with you and the Holy Spirit, one God, throughout all ages.

Epistle: 1 Corinthians 12: 1-11
Gospel: Luke 19: 41-46

Eleventh Sunday after Trinity

O God, your greatness is declared in your loving kindness; graciously grant to us such measure of grace that we, following your commandments, may be worthy of your promises and recipients of your blessing. Through Christ our Lord.
Epistle: 1 Corinthians 15: 1-11
Gospel: Luke18: 9-14

Twelfth Sunday after Trinity

Most mighty and eternal God, you who hear our prayers: embrace us with the abundance of your loving-kindness, and graciously receive our humble petitions, through the merits and mediation of Jesus Christ your only Son, our Lord.

Epistle: 2 Corinthians 3: 1-18
Gospel: Mark 7: 31-37

Thirteenth Sunday after Trinity

Loving and all-powerful God, grant that your faithful people may render you true and unfailing service, that serving you devotedly in this life they may merit the eternal reward of your heavenly promises. Through Christ our Lord.

Epistle: Galatians 3: 16-29
Gospel: Luke 10: 23-37

COLLECTS AND READINGS

Fourteenth Sunday after Trinity

Eternal, most mighty God, increase us in faith, in hope, and in charity; and, that we may attain to the things you have promised, cause us to love your precepts. Through Christ our Lord.

Epistle: Galatians 5: 16-26
Gospel: Luke 17: 11-19

Fifteenth Sunday after Trinity
O Lord, we pray you to imbue your Church with the light of your loving kindness; and grant us your aid, O most holy, that we may ever be kept safe from harm, and guided to the attainment of things profitable to salvation. Through Christ our Lord.

Epistle: Galatians 6: 1-8
Gospel: Matthew 6: 24-34

Sixteenth Sunday after Trinity

O Lord, let your great and unfailing love purify and protect your Church; and because without your help the Church could not continue its work safely and with right intention, uphold it evermore by your goodness and nourish it with your Spirit. Through Jesus Christ your only Son, our Lord, who lives and reigns with you and the same Holy Spirit, one God, throughout all ages.

Epistle: Ephesians 3: 13-21
Gospel: Luke 7: 11-17

COME AND WORSHIP

Seventeenth Sunday after Trinity

May your grace ever go before us, O Lord, and may it follow us, making us continually to aspire to good and righteous works, to the honour and glory of your name. Through Jesus Christ your Son, our Lord, who lives and reigns with you and the Holy Spirit, one God, throughout all ages.

Epistle: Ephesians 4: 1-7
Gospel: Luke 14: 1-11

Eighteenth Sunday after Trinity

O Lord, we pray you to grant your people grace to overcome the enticements of the world and of the flesh, and the deceits of darkness; that with purity of heart and mind they may follow you, the only God. Through Christ our Lord.

Epistle: 1 Corinthians 1: 4-8
Gospel: Matthew 22: 34-46

Nineteenth Sunday after Trinity

O God, without you our soul languishes, and we are unable to please you; of your great love, grant us therefore that your Holy Spirit may in all things be with us, to direct and rule our hearts. Through Jesus Christ your Son, our Lord, who lives and reigns with you and the same Holy Spirit, one God, throughout all ages.

Epistle: Ephesians 4: 17-32
Gospel: Matthew 9: 1-8

COLLECTS AND READINGS

Twentieth Sunday after Trinity

God most mighty, in the abundance of your loving kindness defend us, we pray you, from all harm, and keep us in your light: that we, being ready in both body and soul, may joyfully achieve the goals you set before us. Through Christ our Lord.

Epistle: Ephesians 5: 15-21
Gospel: Matthew 22: 1-14

Twenty-first Sunday after Trinity

Loving Lord, grant to your faithful people pardon and peace, that their failings may be erased, and that they may serve you with confidence and in peace. Through Jesus Christ your Son, our Lord, who lives and reigns with you and the Holy Spirit, one God, throughout all ages.

Epistle: Ephesians 6: 10-20
Gospel: John 4: 46-54

Twenty-Second Sunday after Trinity

O Lord our God, bless as your own appointed foundation for the gathering in of souls to your praise, the Church of Jesus Christ; that its teachings may, by the power of your Holy Spirit, be incisive and honest, its worship sincere and pure and acceptable to you, and the service of its ministers ennobled as an offering for your Son's sake. Through the same Jesus Christ your Son, our Lord, who lives and reigns with you and the same Holy Spirit, one God, throughout all ages.

COME AND WORSHIP

Epistle: Philippians 1: 3-11
Gospel: Matthew: 21-35

Last Sunday after Trinity

Pardon the failings of your people, O Lord, that by your loving kindness they may be delivered from the bondage of sin, and by your grace made worthy of eternal life. Through Jesus Christ your Son, our Lord, who lives and reigns with you and the Holy Spirit, one God, throughout all ages.
Epistle: Colossians 1: 3-20
Gospel: Matthew 9: 10-26

Fourth Sunday before Advent

O Lord, grant that the reality of the mysteries of the faith that our lips utter, be so emplaced in our hearts that we may ever experience their life and their power within our souls. Through Jesus Christ your Son, our Lord, who lives and reigns with you and the Holy Spirit, one God, throughout all ages.

Epistle: Hebrews 9: 1-28
Gospel: Mark 12: 28-34

Third Sunday before Advent

Loving God, may our faithful adherence to your precepts keep us ever within your protection, and make us to have an everlasting reverence for your holy name, and a perfect love of your truth. Through Jesus Christ your Son, our Lord, who lives and reigns with you and the Holy Spirit, one God, throughout all ages.

COLLECTS AND READINGS

Epistle: 1 Thessalonians 4: 13-18
Gospel: Matthew 25: 1-13

Second Sunday before Advent

Grant, O God, that when your only Son, Jesus Christ our Lord, shall come again in power and majesty, we may be found worthy to be made like unto him, to shine with all his saints, in his holy and glorious kingdom. Through the same Jesus Christ our Lord, who lives and reigns with you and the Holy Spirit, one God, throughout all ages.
Epistle: Hebrews 10: 11-25
Gospel: Luke 21: 5-19

Sunday next before Advent

Feast of Christ the King

Most mighty and ever-living God, whose only Son, our Lord Jesus Christ, was assumed into celestial light, to sit upon the throne of heaven and to rule as king: may all things own his royal sway, worshipping him in the beauty of holiness, and proclaiming him King of Glory. Through the same Jesus Christ your Son, our Lord, who lives and reigns with you and the Holy Spirit, one God, throughout all ages.

Epistle: Ephesians 1: 3-23 *or* Revelation 1: 4-8
Gospel: John 18: 33-37

COME AND WORSHIP

SANCTORAL CYCLE

JANUARY

1 - The Naming of the Lord

O God, you established your only Son as the Saviour of humankind, and you decreed that he should be called Jesus: graciously grant us, we pray you, that our reverence for his holy name on earth may lead to our adoration of his countenance in heaven. Through Jesus Christ your Son, our Lord, who lives and reigns with you and the Holy Spirit, one God, throughout all ages.

Epistle: Acts 4: 8-12
Gospel: Luke 2: 21

2 - Basil the Great and Gregory of Nazianzus

O God, by your blessed gift Basil and Gregory came to your people as ministers of everlasting salvation. May they, who have shown us the way of life, by their teachings enlighten our minds and by their example increase our faith. Through Jesus Christ your Son, our Lord, who lives and reigns with you and the Holy Spirit, one God, throughout all ages.

Epistle: 2 Timothy 4: 1-8
Gospel: Matthew 5: 13-19

8 - Gudula

O God our Saviour, hear our prayer, and, as we celebrate this feast of the blessed virgin Gudula,

COLLECTS AND READINGS

fill us with the light of innocence, that we may offer ourselves to you in purity and love. Through Jesus Christ your Son, our Lord, who lives and reigns with you and the Holy Spirit, one God, throughout all ages.

Epistle: 2 Corinthians 10:
Matthew 25: 1-13

13 - Baptism of Christ

(If January 13 is a Sunday, the Feast of the Baptism is transferred to January 14)

Most mighty God, eternal One: the Holy Spirit descended upon Jesus when he was baptised in the Jordan, and your own voice was heard declaring him to be your Son, the delight of your heart; grant, we pray you, that we, your children born of water and the Spirit, may come to share his divinity, who deigned to share our humanity. Through the same Jesus Christ your Son, our Lord, who lives and reigns with you and the same Holy Spirit, one God, throughout all ages.

Epistle: Acts 10: 34-38
Gospel: Mark 1: 7-11

17 – Anthony of Egypt

O Lord: grant us, who this day celebrate the feast of blessed Anthony of Egypt, to live rightly and justly: tempering endeavour with the refreshment of prayer, and exercising moderation in all things. Through Jesus Christ your Son, our Lord, who lives and reigns with you and the Holy Spirit, one God,

COME AND WORSHIP

throughout all ages.

Epistle: 2 Timothy 4: 1-8
Gospel: Matthew 19: 27-29

25 - Conversion of St. Paul

O God, the whole world has been illumined by the teachings of your blessed apostle Paul: grant us, who are celebrating the feast of his conversion, to attain to the light of your glory by following closely the example he has set before us in his life and work. Through Jesus Christ your Son, our Lord, who lives and reigns with you and the Holy Spirit, one God, throughout all ages.

Epistle: Acts 9: 1-22
Gospel: Matthew 19: 27-29

28 - Thomas Aquinas

Lord our God, by whom blessed Thomas, the angelic doctor, came as minister of salvation, to teach your people the mysteries of the faith: graciously grant that we who heed his words may dwell in contemplation of the wonder and holiness of your works. Through Jesus Christ your Son, our Lord, who lives and reigns with you and the Holy Spirit, one God, throughout all ages.

Lesson (Epistle): Proverbs 4: 1-13
Gospel: Matthew 5: 13-19

COLLECTS AND READINGS

FEBRUARY

1 – Brigid of Kildare

O God of our salvation, hear our prayers as we celebrate this feast of the blessed maiden Brigid, bringer of light and awakener of hope; and grant that our hearts and minds may ever be receptive to the splendour of your word, to abound in good works. Through Jesus Christ your Son, our Lord, who lives and reigns with you and the Holy Spirit, one God, throughout all ages.

Epistle: Titus 1: 15-16, 2: 1-15, 3: 1-7
Gospel: John 15: 1-8

2 - The Presentation

Eternal and most mighty God, we pray your majesty, that, as your only Son was presented in the temple in substance of our flesh, so may we be presented to you, with hearts made pure and filled with light, by the same your Son, Jesus Christ our Lord, who lives and reigns with you and the Holy Spirit, one God, throughout all ages.

Epistle: Malachi 3: 1-4
Gospel: Luke 2: 22-32

14 – Cyril and Methodius

O God, may the example of blessed Cyril and Methodius create in us a desire to persevere for the faith at all times, with an unfailing devotion and a most sure belief. Through Jesus Christ your Son, our Lord, who lives and reigns with you and

COME AND WORSHIP

the Holy Spirit, one God, throughout all ages.

Epistle: 2 Thessalonians 2: 13-17
Gospel: John 10: 14-18

23 – Polycarp

O Lord, your blessed martyr Polycarp manifested humility and stoicism in his pilgrimage: may his example be for us an inspiration and a strength. Through Jesus Christ your Son, our Lord, who lives and reigns with you and the Holy Spirit, one God, throughout all ages.

Epistle: 1 Peter 3: 14-18
Gospel: Matthew 10: 16-22

MARCH

1 – David of Wales

O Lord, may the zeal of blessed David in furthering the faith ever be a testimony to inspire your people in their labours and to strengthen them in their pilgrimage. Through Jesus Christ your Son, our Lord, who lives and reigns with you and the Holy Spirit, one God, throughout all ages.

Epistle: Hebrews 12: 1-2
Gospel: Matthew 25: 31-40

2 – Chad of Lichfield

O God, your servant blessed Chad was humble, kindly and devout: may his example encourage us to develop like virtues in our own lives, to the

COLLECTS AND READINGS

honour of your name. Through Jesus Christ your Son, our Lord, who lives and reigns with you and the Holy Spirit, one God, throughout all ages.

Epistle: 1 Corinthians 1: 26-31
Gospel: Matthew 25: 1-13

17 – Patrick of Ireland

O Lord, blessed Patrick was the champion of equality in the society of his time, a man of simplicity and piety and great pastoral endeavour: may his light illumine the faithful and shine brightly throughout today's world as a beacon of hope and justice. Through Jesus Christ your Son, our Lord, who lives and reigns with you and the Holy Spirit, one God, throughout all ages.

Epistle: Hebrews 7: 23-27
Gospel: Matthew 24: 42-47

19 - Joseph of Nazareth

O Lord, on this feast day we honour the memory of blessed Joseph, husband of the Blessed Lady Mary, to whom you entrusted the care of your only Son Jesus. May we who consider the example of his life be as diligent in our own occupations as he was in his, and likewise as aware of the high privileges and consequent responsibilities that fall to us as servants of your household . Through the same Jesus Christ your Son, our Lord, who lives and reigns with you and the Holy Spirit, one God, throughout all ages.

COME AND WORSHIP

Epistle: Colossians 3: 12-15
Gospel: Matthew 13: 54-58

20 – Cuthbert

O God, may the achievements and faith of blessed Cuthbert, whose feast day we are celebrating, bring joy to our hearts, inspiration to our minds and hope to our souls. Through Jesus Christ your Son, our Lord, who lives and reigns with you and the Holy Spirit, one God, throughout all ages.

Epistle: 1 Corinthians 2: 6-16
Gospel: John 17: 18-23

25 - The Annunciation

O Lord, pour forth your grace into our hearts, we pray you, that as we have known the incarnation of your Son Jesus Christ by the word of the angelic messenger, so by his cross and passion may we come to the glory of his resurrection. Through Jesus Christ your Son, our Lord, who lives and reigns with you and the Holy Spirit, one God, throughout all ages.

Reading: Isaiah 7: 10-15
Gospel: Luke 1: 26-38

APRIL

21 – Anselm of Canterbury

O Lord, blessed Anselm wrote searchingly of things unseen, holy and transcendent, and worked tirelessly in your service: may we, who

COLLECTS AND READINGS

acknowledge his understanding and devotion, aspire to live like him with minds open to the guidance of your Holy Spirit and with bodies ready to perform the works you require of us. Through Jesus Christ your only Son, our Lord, who lives and reigns with you and the same Holy Spirit, one God, throughout all ages.

Epistle: 1 Corinthians 2: 6-16
Gospel: John 17: 18-23

23 – George of England

O God, your warrior blessed George fought the good fight, faithfully defending your people and attaining to the crown of martyrdom: may we who journey through this world be defended by the same power that he showed forth, even the strength of your right arm, O Lord God of Hosts. Through Jesus Christ your Son, our Lord, who lives and reigns with you and the Holy Spirit, one God, throughout all ages.

Epistle: 1 Peter 4: 12-19
Gospel: Mark 8: 34-38

25 – Mark, Evangelist, Martyr

O God, you gave to your holy Church the celestial doctrine of blessed Mark: give us grace, we pray you, that we waver not in that faith, but that our hearts and minds may be securely founded in the truth of your holy Gospel. Through Jesus Christ your Son, our Lord, who lives and reigns with you and the Holy Spirit, one God, throughout all ages.

COME AND WORSHIP

Epistle: Ephesians 4: 7-16
Gospel: John 15: 1-11

29 – Catherine of Siena

O Lord, for whom blessed Catherine of Siena laboured courageously and in holiness: grant that we may, like her, see Christ in our brothers and sisters, and in the life of your Church; and that we may come to know him, the crucified, as the supreme manifestation of your love for us. Through the same Jesus Christ your Son, our Lord, who lives and reigns with you and the Holy Spirit, one God, throughout all ages.

Epistle: 2 Corinthians 6: 1-10
Gospel: Matthew 6: 24-33

MAY

1 – Phillip and James, Apostles

O God, in true knowledge of whom is eternal life: grant us perfectly to know your Son Jesus Christ to be the way, the truth and the life; that walking in the steps of blessed Philip and blessed James we may follow the path that leads to your presence. Through the same Jesus Christ your Son, our Lord, who lives and reigns with you and the Holy Spirit, one God, throughout all ages.

Epistle: James 1: 1-12
Gospel: John 14: 1-14

COLLECTS AND READINGS

2 – Athanasius of Alexandria

O God, whose blessed servant Athanasius affirmed that your image within us, marred by our failings, is to be restored to its shining, unsullied and original splendour: grant us, we pray you, that we may truly become your children through adoption by Christ, so to participate in the outpouring of your grace. Through the same Jesus Christ your Son, our Lord, who lives and reigns with you and the Holy Spirit, one God, throughout all ages.

Epistle: Acts 15: 7-21
Gospel: John 15: 9-11

14 – Matthias, Apostle, Martyr

O God of power, who chose blessed Matthias to be of the number of the apostles: grant that your Church may always be defended and guided by faithful and true ministers. Through Jesus Christ your Son, our Lord, who lives and reigns with you and the Holy Spirit, one God, throughout all ages.

Epistle: Acts 1: 15-26
Matthew 11: 25-31

31 - The Visitation

O Lord, bestow upon us the gift of divine grace, as we call to mind that the beginning of our salvation was in the childbearing of blessed Mary; that we, who on this festival of the Visitation proclaim, My soul magnifies the Lord, my spirit rejoices in God my Saviour, may find increase of peace within our souls. Through Christ our Lord.

COME AND WORSHIP

Reading: Song of Songs 2: 8-14
Gospel: Luke 1: 39-47

JUNE

1 – Justin, Martyr

O God, may the example of blessed Justin, teacher and advocate of the faith, encourage in us strength of heart and mind as we live our lives according to your precepts. Through Jesus Christ your Son, our Lord, who lives and reigns with you and the Holy Spirit, one God, throughout all ages.

Epistle: 1 Peter 3: 14-22
Gospel: Matthew 10: 16-22

9 – Columba of Iona

O Lord, as we celebrate this feast of blessed Columba, may our hearts be enlarged in love, and our sense of responsibility deepened, towards all for whom we bear responsibility of guidance, care or tutelage. Through Jesus Christ your Son, our Lord, who lives and reigns with you and the Holy Spirit, one God, throughout all ages.

Epistle: 1 Thessalonians 2: 2-12
Gospel: Matthew 5: 13-16

11 – Barnabas, Martyr

O Lord, you imbued blessed Barnabas with eminent gifts of the Holy Spirit: may we also be imbued with such measure of power as you desire for us, and with the grace to use it aright, to the

COLLECTS AND READINGS

honour and glory of your name. Through Jesus Christ our Lord.

Epistle: Acts 11: 22-30
Gospel: John 15: 12-16

22 – Alban, Martyr

Grant us, O Lord, on this feast of blessed Alban, always to remain true to our convictions, and by that same constancy to proclaim the faith with true courage. Through Jesus Christ your Son, our Lord, who lives and reigns with you and the Holy Spirit, one God, throughout all ages.

Epistle: Revelation 7: 13-17
Gospel: Luke 12: 2-12

24 - Birth of John the Baptist

O God, by whose divine intention blessed John the Baptist was wonderfully born, and became the forerunner of your Son: cause us, we pray you, so to follow John's teaching and his holiness of life that we may be found worthy to receive the Lord Jesus and to acclaim him as Light of the World. Through the same Jesus Christ your Son, our Lord, who lives and reigns with you and the Holy Spirit, one God, throughout all ages.

Reading: Isaiah 40: 1-11
Gospel: Luke 1: 57-80

27 – Cyril of Alexandria

O God, blessed Cyril contended with error, and

COME AND WORSHIP

gained victory for the truth of your word, teaching the faith clearly and conscientiously, and adding to the wisdom of your Church: grant that we, like him, may bear unfaltering witness to the mysteries of the faith, and enlarge, to whatever degree, the wisdom of your household by the holiness and purity of our thoughts and deeds. Through Jesus Christ your Son, our Lord, who lives and reigns with you and the Holy Spirit, one God, throughout all ages.

Epistle: 2 Timothy 4: 1-8
Gospel: Matthew 5: 13-19

28 – Irenaeus

O Lord, your blessed confessor Irenaeus worked impartially for peace and unity among your people, and followed the banner of truth in his significant teachings: grant us a like disposition, we pray, that we may work for the healing of the nations, promoting harmony where discord holds sway, and understanding where misunderstanding abounds. Through Jesus Christ your Son, our Lord, who lives and reigns with you and the Holy Spirit, one God, throughout all ages.

Epistle: 2 Timothy 3: 14-17
Gospel: Matthew 10: 28-32

29 – Peter and Paul, Apostles, Martyrs

O God, you have consecrated this day by the martyrdom of blessed Peter and blessed Paul. Grant that your holy Church may in all things follow their precepts conscientiously and with

COLLECTS AND READINGS

understanding, in accordance with her heritage. Through Jesus Christ your Son, our Lord, who lives and reigns with you and the Holy Spirit, one God, throughout all ages.

Epistle: Acts 12: 1-11
Gospel: Matthew 16: 13-19

JULY

3 - Thomas, Apostle, Martyr

O God, whose servant blessed Thomas at first doubted your Son's resurrection, but who then confessed him with his whole heart: grant us to have no shadow of doubt, but only true and perfect faith in your Christ, that we may stand before you unashamed. Through the same Jesus Christ your Son, our Lord, who lives and reigns with you and the Holy Spirit, one God, throughout all ages.

Epistle: Ephesians 2: 19-22
Gospel: John 20: 24-31

11 - Benedict of Nursia

O Lord, as we celebrate this feast of blessed Benedict, may our powers of body and soul be united in aspiration to serve you in holiness, and in desire to treat our brothers and sisters with justice and equity, to the honour and glory of your name. Through Jesus Christ your Son, our Lord, who lives and reigns with you and the Holy Spirit, one God, throughout all ages.

COME AND WORSHIP

Reading: Proverbs 3: 1-12
Gospel: Matthew 19: 27-29

22 – Mary Magdalene

Loving God, grant us by your grace never to fall short of the mark you have set for us; but should it be on occasion that we offend against your divine majesty, then let it so be that by true repentance, after the example of blessed Mary Magdalene, and by lively faith, we may obtain remission of our sins, through the merits of your Son, our Lord Jesus Christ, who lives and reigns with you and the Holy Spirit, one God, throughout all ages.

Epistle: 2 Corinthians 5: 14-19
Gospel: John 20: 11-18

25 – James, Apostle, Martyr

Grant, O God, that even as blessed James, leaving his father and all that he had, was at once obedient to the summons of your Son Jesus Christ and followed him; so we, forsaking all worldly interests, may be ready without delay to follow your commandments. Through the same Jesus Christ your Son, our Lord, who lives and reigns with you and the Holy Spirit, one God, throughout all ages.

Epistle: Acts 11: 27-30, 12: 1-2
Gospel: Matthew 20: 20-28

COLLECTS AND READINGS

AUGUST

6 - The Transfiguration

O God, in the glorious transfiguration of your only Son you confirmed the mystery of faith, and proclaimed, in the voice from the cloud, our perfect adoption as your children. In your loving kindness, we pray you, make us co-heirs with the king of glory, participant in his light. Through the same Jesus Christ your Son, our Lord, who lives and reigns with you and the Holy Spirit, one God, throughout all ages.

Epistle: 1 John 3: 1-3
Gospel: Mark 9: 2-9

10 - Laurence, Martyr

Mighty God, may the compassion, generosity and steadfastness of blessed Laurence your martyr be to us a witness of the faith, and may his example encourage in us a noble generosity, in your name, towards the needy. Through Jesus Christ your Son, our Lord, who lives and reigns with you and the Holy Spirit, one God, throughout all ages.

Epistle: Revelation 7: 13-17
Gospel: John 12: 24-26

11 - Clare of Assisi

O Lord, your handmaiden, the blessed Clare, loved all your creatures and the beauties of your world; and her inner life was a song of simplicity and devotion, reflected outwardly in the austerity and

COME AND WORSHIP

poverty enjoined by her order. May this her feast day ever be a light to our minds, and may it inspire us to discover that which is noblest and best within ourselves and in the external world. Through Jesus Christ your Son, our Lord, who lives and reigns with you and the Holy Spirit, one God, throughout all ages.

Epistle: 2 Corinthians 10: 17-18
Gospel: Matthew 25: 1-13

15 - The Assumption of Blessed Mary

Most mighty and eternal God, you have taken into your glory, body, soul and spirit, immaculate Mary, the Mother of your Son. Grant, we pray you, that our aspiration being always to things supernal, we too may come to share in your glory. Through the same Jesus Christ your Son, our Lord, who lives and reigns with you and the Holy Spirit, one God, throughout all ages.

Reading: Psalm 45: 10-17
Gospel: Luke 1: 41-50

20 - Bernard of Clairvaux

O Lord our God, may the works of blessed Bernard, pillar of the temple, lead us to illumination of heart and mind, and glory of soul, through our living devotion to your most holy precepts. Through Jesus Christ your Son, our Lord, who lives and reigns with you and the Holy Spirit, one God, throughout all ages.

COLLECTS AND READINGS

Epistle: 1 John 4: 7-21
Gospel: Matthew 5: 13-19

24 - Bartholomew, Apostle, Martyr

O God, mighty and eternal, who gave to blessed
Bartholomew the grace to believe your word truly
and to preach it with conviction: grant to your
Church, we pray you, such love of the word that
he believed, and such grace to teach and to
receive the same, that your glorious name may
thereby be worthily magnified. Through Jesus
Christ your Son, our Lord, who lives and reigns
with you and the Holy Spirit, one God, throughout
all ages.

Epistle: Acts 5: 12-16
Gospel: Luke 22: 24-30

28 - Augustine of Hippo

O God, your servant blessed Augustine gave to
your Church many treasures of theology, the
beauty and cogency of which remain undiminished
to this day: grant that our response in heart and
soul to his good and perceptive teachings may
assist us in our homeward journey to your eternal
light. Through Jesus Christ your Son, our Lord,
who lives and reigns with you and the Holy Spirit,
one God, throughout all ages.

2 Timothy 4: 1-8
Matthew 5: 13-19

COME AND WORSHIP

31 – Aidan of Lindisfarne

O Lord, blessed Aidan was famed for his patience and humility, for his compassion, for his care of the poor, and for his life of prayer: may we seek to emulate his example by developing and fostering like virtues in our own lives, to the honour of your name. Through Jesus Christ your Son, our Lord, who lives and reigns with you and the Holy Spirit, one God, throughout all ages.

Epistle: Ephesians 3: 14-21
Gospel: Matthew 28: 16-20

SEPTEMBER

3 – Gregory the Great

O Lord most high, with your undoubted guidance your servant Gregory the Great demonstrated understanding and skill in his governance of your household, and left to your faithful people a divinely-inspired legacy of beauty and lasting worth : may our own endeavours in this life, with the aid of your grace, be undertaken with due sense of responsibility, with insight, and with care, that we in our turn, and in our own fashion, may leave a legacy both honourable and estimable. Through Jesus Christ your Son, our Lord, who lives and reigns with you and the Holy Spirit, one God, throughout all ages.

Epistle: 1 Corinthians 3: 5-11
Gospel: Matthew 13: 47-52

COLLECTS AND READINGS

13 – John Chrysostom

O Lord, among the treasures left to your faithful people by blessed John Chrysostom was his affirmation of the value of holy scripture in its literal meaning, and the enduring and potent relevance of those same holy writings in regard to the conditions of the age: grant, we pray you, that we, your servants, ever listening to your word in this present age, may discern the spiritual truths proclaimed therein, and thus receive inspiration and guidance proper to our times. Through Jesus Christ your Son, our Lord, who lives and reigns with you and the Holy Spirit, one God, throughout all ages.

Epistle: 1 Timothy 3: 1-13
Gospel: Luke 7: 11-17

14 - Holy Cross Day

O God, every year we are gladdened by the solemnity of the Exaltation of the Holy Cross; of your great loving kindness, grant that we who have known the mystery of the redemption in this world may receive the rewards thereof in the heavenly realm. Through Jesus Christ your Son, our Lord, who lives and reigns with you and the Holy Spirit, one God, throughout all ages.

Epistle: Philippians 2: 5-11
Gospel: John 12: 31-36

16 – Euphemia, Martyr

O Lord most high, your great martyr blessed

COME AND WORSHIP

Euphemia stood firm in the faith, and passed from this world into the light of your glory with courage and honour. Grant, we pray you, that we, like her, may be so strongly established in the faith, that we never fail in loving devotion to you. Through Jesus Christ your Son, our Lord, who lives and reigns with you and the Holy Spirit, one God, throughout all ages.

Epistle: Revelation 7: 13-17
Gospel: Luke 12: 2-12

17 – Hildegard of Bingen

O God, imbued with the flame of your love, blessed Hildegard became a shining light in your Church: grant, we pray you, that we also may be imbued with that sacred flame, ever to walk in your ways as children of the light. Through Jesus Christ your Son, our Lord, who lives and reigns with you and the Holy Spirit, one God, throughout all ages.

Epistle: 2 Corinthians 6: 1-10
Gospel: Matthew 6: 24-33

21 – Matthew, Apostle, Martyr

Most mighty God, you called blessed Matthew from monetary concerns to be an apostle and evangelist: grant us grace, we pray you, to renounce all covetousness and excessive love of wealth, and like him to follow in the footsteps of your Son Jesus Christ, who lives and reigns with you and the Holy Spirit, one God, throughout all ages.

COLLECTS AND READINGS

Epistle: 2 Corinthians 4: 1-6
Gospel: Matthew 9: 9-13

29 - Michael and All Angels

Eternal God, in wonderful fashion you provided one ministry for your angels and another for us, your sons and daughters: of your loving kindness, be pleased to grant that those holy ones, the messengers of your will who serve you in the celestial realms, may be our guardians on earth. Through Jesus Christ your Son, our Lord, who lives and reigns with you and the Holy Spirit, one God, throughout all ages.

Epistle: Revelation 12: 7-12
Gospel: Matthew 28: 1-6

30 - Jerome

O God, you have illuminated your Church by the witness and works of blessed Jerome: pour forth upon her, your Church, the abundance of your blessing, we pray you, that she may always have faithful advocates to proclaim the truth of your salvation by their life and teaching. Through Jesus Christ your Son, our Lord, who lives and reigns with you and the Holy Spirit, one God, throughout all ages.

Epistle: 2 Timothy 4: 1-8
Gospel: Matthew 5: 13-19

OCTOBER

4 – Francis of Assisi

O God, blessed Francis recognised your essential goodness and life, the activity of your Holy Spirit, in all of creation: grant that we, following his example, may, by the gift of your grace, look beyond the form of things to recognise their true life in you. Through Jesus Christ your Son, our Lord, who lives and reigns with you and the same Holy Spirit, one God, throughout all ages.

Epistle: Galatians 6: 14-18
Gospel: Matthew 11: 25-30

12 – Symeon the New Theologian

O Lord, through his mystic contemplation blessed Symeon perceived the shining light and scintillant flame of your Holy Spirit, and entered into your presence and knew your powers: may we, in the deep yearnings of our meditations and prayers draw ever closer to you, that we too may in reverence receive you and enter into the beauty of your light. Through Jesus Christ your Son, our Lord, who lives and reigns with you and the same Holy Spirit, one God, throughout all ages.

Epistle: 1 Corinthians 2: 6-16
Gospel: John 17: 18-23

13 – Edward, Confessor

O Lord, blessed Edward ruled his people, your faithful children, with justice and equity, with

COLLECTS AND READINGS

compassion and peace, with generosity of spirit and with kindness: grant, we pray you, that we may so order our own lives according to these good and honourable things that we may be judged worthy to inherit eternal life. Through our Lord Jesus Christ.

Epistle: Hebrews 12: 1-2
Gospel: Matthew 25: 31-40

15 – Teresa of Avila

O God, by your grace blessed Teresa bore faithful and true witness to the faith by her devotion and achievements: grant us, we pray, that following her holy example, we may be found ready for the coming of the bridegroom, to enter with him into the marriage feast. Through the same Jesus Christ your Son, our Lord, who lives and reigns with you and the Holy Spirit, one God, throughout all ages.

Epistle: 2 Corinthians 10: 17-18, 11: 1-2
Gospel: Matthew 25: 1-13

17 – Ignatius of Antioch, Martyr

O Lord our God, blessed Ignatius the God-bearer, the advocate of unity in and through the Eucharist, served your Church with zeal and devotion: may we, like him, come to know the presence and power of Christ within us, that as true Christians we too may be accounted God-bearers. Through the same Jesus Christ your Son, our Lord, who lives and reigns with you and the Holy Spirit, one God, throughout all ages.

COME AND WORSHIP

Epistle: 1 Peter 3: 14-22
Gospel: Matthew 10: 16-22

18 - Luke, Evangelist, Martyr

Most mighty God, you called blessed Luke to be an evangelist and physician of the soul: grant, we pray you, that the medicine of the doctrine he transmitted may be a salutary remedy for the perfecting of our souls. Through Jesus Christ your Son, our Lord, who lives and reigns with you and the Holy Spirit, one God, throughout all ages.

Epistle: 2 Timothy 4: 1-8
Gospel: Luke 7: 36-50

28 - Simon and Jude, Apostles, Martyrs

God of power, you built your Church upon the foundation of the apostles and prophets, Jesus Christ himself being the head corner-stone: grant us, we pray you, so to be bonded together in unity of spirit by their teaching, that we may be made a holy temple acceptable to you. Through Jesus Christ your Son, our Lord, who lives and reigns with you and the Holy Spirit, one God, throughout all ages.

Epistle: Revelation 21: 9-14
Gospel: John 15: 17-27

NOVEMBER

1 - All Saints' Day

Most mighty God, you have united your people in

295

COLLECTS AND READINGS

one communion in the mystical body of your Son Jesus Christ: grant us grace so to follow your blessed saints in all virtuous and holy living, we pray you, that we may be found worthy to receive the blessed and joyful reward prepared for those who truly love you. Through Jesus Christ your Son, our Lord, who lives and reigns with you and the Holy Spirit, one God, throughout all ages.

Epistle: Revelation 7: 2-4, 9-12
Gospel: Matthew 5: 1-12

2 - All Souls' Day

O God, creator and redeemer of the faithful, grant to the souls of your faithful departed children the perfect remission of their sins; and of your great and loving kindness, bring them into the place of happiness, of blessed peace and of shining light. Through Christ our Lord.

Epistle: 1 Corinthians 15: 51-57
Gospel: John 6: 51-55

10 - Leo the Great

O God, light of the faithful and shepherd of souls, you established your servant blessed Leo as a great priest in your Church, to feed your sheep by his teaching and to guide them by his example; through him you revealed, plainly and directly, deep and ageless mysteries of the faith, so that ambiguity, misunderstanding or dissension should never have cause to arise through succeeding years. Grant us, we pray you, to keep in its essential purity the faith which he cherished and

COME AND WORSHIP

transmitted, and to guard the same with our hearts and minds, our words and our deeds. Through Jesus Christ your Son, our Lord, who lives and reigns with you and the Holy Spirit, one God, throughout all ages.

Epistle: 1 Corinthians 2: 6-16
Gospel: John 17: 18-23

14 – Gregory Palamas

O God, by your Holy Spirit you bestow on some the gift of wisdom, on others the gift of knowledge, and on others the gift of faith: for the gifts of grace manifested in your servant Gregory, we thank you and we praise you, and we pray that your Church may never be without such blessings. Through Jesus Christ your Son, our Lord, who lives and reigns with you and the same Holy Spirit, one God, throughout all ages.

Epistle: Philippians 4: 4-9
Gospel: Luke 6: 17-23

20 – Edmund, Martyr

O God, by whose grace and power blessed Edmund accepted martyrdom with an unshakeable faith: grant us, we pray you, to stand firm, in love of you, through all adversities that may beset us. Through Jesus Christ your Son, our Lord, who lives and reigns with you and the Holy Spirit, one God, throughout all ages.

Epistle: 1 Peter 4: 12-19
Gospel: Mark 8: 34-38

COLLECTS AND READINGS

22 – Cecilia, Martyr

Lord most holy, most loving, you endued the blessed Cecilia with grace to bear witness to your truth, and to remain faithful to you even unto a martyr's death: grant that we may draw strength from the inspiration of her courage and resolve, that we may never be ashamed to confess you, but may ever proudly proclaim your greatness and your glory. Through Jesus Christ your Son, our Lord, who lives and reigns with you and the Holy Spirit, one God, throughout all ages.

Epistle: 2 Timothy 2: 8-15
Gospel: John 15: 1-7

30 – Andrew, Apostle, Martyr

O Lord, blessed Andrew heard the summons of your Son to follow him, and by your grace readily assented thereto: grant to us, that, being summoned by your holy word, we also may arise and follow your Son, to give ourselves wholly to you in fulfillment of your will. Through the same Jesus Christ your Son, our Lord, who lives and reigns with you and the Holy Spirit, one God, throughout all ages.

Epistle: Romans 10: 9-21
Gospel: Matthew 4: 18-22

DECEMBER

7 – Ambrose of Milan

O God, you have illuminated your Church through

COME AND WORSHIP

the teachings and life of blessed Ambrose, defender of the faith and elucidator of your mysteries: shine in our hearts, we pray you, that we too may sound your praises and proclaim the words of life. Through Jesus Christ your Son, our Lord, who lives and reigns with you and the Holy Spirit, one God, throughout all ages.

Epistle: 2 Timothy 4: 1-8
Gospel: Matthew 5: 13-19

14 – John of the Cross

O Lord most tender, most close, blessed John advocated asceticism and spoke of the purification of the soul by divine grace, teaching also that only by fullness of faith and true love of you is the soul enabled to attain to its original splendour and to dwell within the light of your presence. Grant us, most holy, thus to advance in your ways, that we may enter into the flame of your undying glory. Through Christ our Lord..

Reading: Isaiah 48: 17-19
Gospel: Matthew 11: 16-19

26 – Stephen, Proto-martyr

O Lord our God, blessed Stephen prayed to you for those who were about to kill him. May we, being filled with the Holy Spirit and guided by the example of your first martyr, learn to love and to bless in your name those who would be our enemies. Through Jesus Christ your Son, our Lord, who lives and reigns with you and the same Holy Spirit, one God, throughout all ages.

COLLECTS AND READINGS

Epistle: Acts 7: 55-60
Gospel: Matthew 23: 34-39

27 - John, Apostle and Evangelist

Lord of love, bathe your Church in your holy light, that being enlightened by the doctrine of blessed John it may so walk in the light of your truth that it shall, at the last, attain to the light of eternal life. Through Jesus Christ your Son, our Lord, who lives and reigns with you and the Holy Spirit, one God, throughout all ages.

Epistle: 1 John 1: 1-7
Gospel: John 3: 1-8

28 - The Holy Innocents

God of all power, parent of us all, on this feast day of your Holy Innocents, we stand before you as your sons and daughters. Cleanse us of all unworthiness, and strengthen us by your grace, we pray you, that by our own childlike innocence and simplicity of faith, we may glorify your holy name. Through Jesus Christ your Son, our Lord, who lives and reigns with you and the Holy Spirit, one God, throughout all ages.

Epistle: Revelation 14: 1-5
Gospel: Matthew 2: 13-18

REQUIEM MASSES

Funeral Mass

COME AND WORSHIP

Most loving God, we pray you, on behalf of the soul of your servant N, whom you have called from the life of this world to greater life in you: let your saints and holy ones receive him/her, and let your holy angels lead him/her home to paradise: for his/her hope and trust were set firmly in you, and in your light shall he/she see light. Through Christ our Lord.

Epistle: Revelation 22: 1-5
Gospel: John 14: 1-6

Anniversary Mass

O God, Lord of loving kindness, we pray you to give to the soul of your servant N, the anniversary of whose passing into the greater life we are celebrating, a place of refreshment, of blessed peace, and of glorious light. Through Christ our Lord.

Epistle: Revelation 14: 13
Gospel: John 6: 37-40

Daily Mass

Hear the voice of our prayer, O Lord, and in your great and loving kindness regard the soul of your servant N: admit him/her, we ask you, into the company of all your holy ones in the place of light and peace. Through Jesus Christ your Son, our Lord, who lives and reigns with you and the Holy Spirit, one God, throughout all ages.

Epistle: Revelation 14: 13
Gospel: John 6: 51-55

COLLECTS AND READINGS

VOTIVE MASSES

The Sick

God most mighty and ever-living, eternal salvation of believers, hear our prayer, and pour forth the abundance of your loving kindness upon your servants who desire to be healed: may they be restored in life and refreshed in spirit, that they may praise your gracious acts in the assembly of the faithful. Through Jesus Christ your Son, our Lord, who lives and reigns with you and the Holy Spirit, one God, throughout all ages.

Epistle: James 5: 13-16
Gospel: Matthew 8: 5-13

The Angels

O God of majesty, triumphant God, before whose glory the angels of light veil their faces; God of all wisdom, omniscient God, whom myriads of angels do serve; God of all power, loving God, to whom angelic hosts continually do cry 'Holy, Holy, Holy, Lord God almighty, which was, and is, and is to come': graciously grant that those messengers of your word whose ministries you have wonderfully ordained and who attend you in the celestial regions, may be our guardians on earth. Through Jesus Christ your Son, our Lord, who lives and reigns with you and the Holy Spirit, one God, throughout all ages.

Epistle: Revelation 5: 11-14
Gospel: John 1: 47-51

COME AND WORSHIP

Propagation of the Faith

O God, whose desire it is that all people should have knowledge of the truth and so come to salvation, send forth, we pray you, workers into your harvest, that they may proclaim your word with fullness of faith, so sending it forth that its glory may be manifested, and that all the nations may thereby come to know you, the one true God, and him you have sent, Jesus Christ your Son our Lord, who lives and reigns with you and the Holy Spirit, one God, throughout all ages.

Epistle: 1 Timothy 2: 1-7
Gospel: Matthew 9: 35-38

Christian Unity

O Lord our God, of your great love fill all Christian people with the grace of your own oneness, that, while rightly owning diversity in inessentials, they may both know and show forth unity in the essentials of the faith. Through Jesus Christ your Son, our Lord, who lives and reigns with you and the Holy Spirit, one God, throughout all ages.

Epistle: Ephesians 4: 1-21
Gospel: John 14: 23-29

Peace

O God, from whom all holy desires, all good counsels, and all just works do proceed, give unto your servants that peace which the world cannot give: that our hearts being dedicated to your commandments, and the fear of our enemies

COLLECTS AND READINGS

being removed, we may pass our times in tranquility under your protection. Through Jesus Christ your Son, our Lord, who lives and reigns with you and the Holy Spirit, one God, throughout all ages.

Epistle: Philippians 4: 6-9
Gospel: John 20: 19-23

The Holy Spirit

Almighty God, to whom all hearts are open, all desires known, and from whom no secret is hidden, cleanse the thoughts of our hearts by the inspiration of your Holy Spirit, that we may perfectly love you and worthily magnify your holy name. Through Christ our Lord.

Epistle: Acts 8: 14-17
Gospel: John 14: 15-21

The Most Precious Blood of our Lord Jesus Christ

Eternal and most mighty God, in accordance with your will, your only Son redeemed the world by the shedding of his most precious blood: grant us, we pray you, that we may so venerate that blood, the wondrous price of our salvation, that we may be defended against all ills of this world, and that we may, in the heavenly places, for ever rejoice in the fruits of your Son's atonement. Through the same Jesus Christ your Son, our Lord, who lives and reigns with you and the Holy Spirit, one God, throughout all ages.

COME AND WORSHIP

Epistle: 1 Peter 1: 17-21
Gospel: Luke 22: 39-44

The Blessed Lady Mary

O Lord our God, blessed Mary assented to your will, and was imbued with fullness of grace in the beauty of holiness. Grant to us, your servants, we pray you, so to accord with what you desire of us, that, inspired by the glorious faith of the mother of our Lord, we may dwell in concord with you, to the perpetual health of soul and body and to the fulfillment of our destined purpose. Through the same Jesus Christ your Son, our Lord, who lives and reigns with you and the Holy Spirit, one God, throughout all ages.

Alternative Collect:

O God, may the example of the blessed Lady Mary, the mother of the Lord, fill our souls with the sweet fragrance of joy as we reflect with thanks upon her acceptance of your will, and upon her devoted and loving support of your Son. Through the same Jesus Christ your only Son, our Lord, who lives and reigns with you and the Holy Spirit, one God, throughout all ages.

Reading: Song of Songs 2: 8-14
Gospel: Luke 1: 26-28

PREMISES OF THE FAITH

COME AND WORSHIP

PREMISES OF THE FAITH

1 The Holy Trinity, One God
2 The Children of God
3 Sin and Salvation
4 Jesus the Christ
5 The Creed
6 The Holy Bible
7 The Church
8 The Communion of Saints
9 The Ministry of the Laity
10 The Ministry of those in Holy Orders
11 Prayer
12 The Sacraments
13 Adoption in the Beloved
14 The Great Assurance

1 - The Holy Trinity, One God

The central Christian dogma that the one God exists in three Persons and one substance, Father, Son, and Holy Spirit. The God who reveals Himself to mankind is one God equally in three distinct modes of existence, yet remains one through all eternity.

The Concise Oxford Dictionary of the Christian Church

1 – In the divine nature, the unity of the Godhead, there are three Persons, the Father, the Son, and the Holy Spirit. This is the Holy Trinity.

2 - The three Persons are entirely distinct from one another in their relations of origin: the Father

309

PREMISES OF THE FAITH

generates; the Son is begotten of the Father by an eternal generation; the Holy Spirit proceeds by an eternal procession from the Father and the Son.

3 - But all are co-eternal and co-equal. All are uncreated and all-powerful. All have always existed. All are the one divine nature, one God. One God in three Persons, the consubstantial Trinity, each Person being entirely God.

4 - The Father is entirely in the Son and entirely in the Holy Spirit. The Son is entirely in the Father and entirely in the Holy Spirit. The Holy Spirit is entirely in the Father and entirely in the Son.

5 - Even as the divine Persons are one in their nature, so are they one in their operation. But within the common action, each of the Persons shows forth what is proper and unique to them in the Trinity.

6 - The First Person of the Trinity, God the Father, the maker of all things visible and invisible, the fount of life, light and holiness. The Omnipotent Lord. The Father is Truth and Love. Creation is especially to be attributed to God the Father, but it remains that Father, Son and Holy Spirit are together the indivisible principle of creation. The creative action of Son and Holy Spirit is inseparably one with that of the Father.

7 - The Second Person of the Trinity, God the Son, the Logos or "Creative Word" through whom all things were made, Holy Wisdom, the Redeemer, the Image of the Father, the one who reveals God's nature to us. The Son is the eternal focus of

COME AND WORSHIP

the Father's love, and mediator of the Father's love in creation and redemption.

8 - The Third Person of the Trinity, God the Holy Spirit, the Sanctifier, the Life-giver, the Breath of God, Goodness, God at work in the universe and in our souls. The Holy Spirit, called the 'Spirit of Glory' and the 'Spirit of Christ', is the very Life of the worlds. We approach the Father, through Christ, in the power of the Holy Spirit.

9 - God is the source and goal of all evolutionary progress.

2 - The Children of God

1 - Children are we, all of one parentage; sons and daughters of God our Father and Mother.

2 - Body, soul and spirit, we are part of God's universe in its material and spiritual levels.

3 - The universe itself, material and spiritual, is the work of a single divine being: God, who is immanent and transcendent, who creates, sustains and directs it.

4 - All the worlds, the concourse of stars, the stellar galaxies, belong to God, their creator. We are privileged to be participants in this earth, our world, and it is our responsibility to care for it as stewards in accordance with God's purposes.

5 - We have a rational mind, a conscience, and self-awareness. We have the power of self-

PREMISES OF THE FAITH

determination. We are free to make choices: to love, to labour, to create, to reason, to live in harmony with God and nature, and to seek to progress spiritually.

6 - We have the perfect right to freedom of conscience, thought, interpretation and inquiry in regard to all matters of religion and belief.

6 - Our inner being, our spiritual nature, is made in the image of God.

7 - We have the potential to experience the presence of God, to grow in God's love, and to attain mystical oneness with God.

3 - Sin and Salvation

1 - Sin is, ultimately, sin against God; a seeking of spiritual and moral autonomy which is founded in unbelief and rebellion. In sin we seek to do our own will rather than the will of God.

2 - In committing sin we 'miss the mark', we fall short of the standard which is required of us by God and which is fitting to the proper dignity of human nature.

3 - By sin we create disharmony in our relationship with others and with all creation, we cloud the divine image within us, and we damage our interaction with God.

4 - Salvation is the act of God which breaks the bondage of sin, the act which frees us and

COME AND WORSHIP

restores us to wholeness.

'...... God is eternal blessedness, undying life, unfading light. God is love: Father, Son and Holy Spirit. God freely wills to communicate the glory of his blessed life. Such is the 'plan of his loving kindness', conceived by the Father before the foundation of the world, in his beloved Son: 'He destined us in love to be his sons' and 'to be conformed to the image of his Son', through 'the spirit of sonship'. This plan is a 'grace [which] was given to us in Christ Jesus before the ages began', stemming immediately from Trinitarian love. It unfolds in the work of creation, the whole history of salvation after the fall, and the missions of the Son and the Spirit, which are continued in the mission of the Church.'

Catechism of the Catholic Church,
The Divine Works and the Trinitarian Missions

4 - Jesus the Christ

1 - The Son, the Second Person of the Trinity, became incarnate so that we might be adopted through him as Children of God. By an act of God he took flesh from the womb of the virgin Mary and lived and taught among us as Jesus, the Christ of God.

2 - By the example of his life, and the transformative light of his teaching, Christ showed the ways of peace and holiness, and the love, the power and the will of God.

3 - Our salvation is effected through the Lord Jesus Christ, whose passion and death was the perfect and atoning sacrifice for the sins of the

PREMISES OF THE FAITH

whole world, the very offering whereby we are reconciled with God and our souls are regenerated.

4 - By rising from the dead, Christ triumphed over death, bestowing the fullness of the New Life, of Life in Abundance, upon all believers.

5 - All who are baptised become living members of Christ's Mystical Body, the Church, and share in his resurrection.

6 - Christ gave us this twofold summary of the Law: You shall love the Lord your God with all your heart, with all your soul, and with all your mind. You shall love your neighbour as yourself. Christ also gave us the New Commandment: that we should love one another even as he loved us. It is the duty and joy of Christians to live according to these great guiding principles.

5 - The Creed

1 - We hold to the *Nicene Creed*, the creed of the Universal Church, as the traditional definition of our catholic faith.

'We believe in one God, the Father almighty, maker of heaven and earth, and of all things visible and invisible.

'We believe in one Lord, Jesus Christ, the only begotten Son of God, born of the Father before all ages. God from God, Light from Light, true God from true God, begotten not made, of one

COME AND WORSHIP

substance with the Father. Through him all things were made. For us and for our salvation he came down from heaven. By the power of the Holy Spirit he became incarnate from the Virgin Mary, and was made man. He was crucified for us under Pontius Pilate. He suffered and was buried. On the third day he rose again according to the scriptures. He ascended into heaven and is seated at the right hand of the Father. He will come again in glory to judge both the living and the dead, and his kingdom shall have no end.

'We believe in the Holy Spirit, the Lord and giver of life, who proceeds from the Father and Son, who together with the Father and the Son is worshipped and glorified, who has spoken through the prophets. We believe in one, holy, catholic and apostolic Church. We acknowledge one baptism for the remission of sins. And we look for the resurrection of the dead, and the life of the world to come. Amen.'

2 - We accept the *Apostles' Creed*, as sufficient baptismal affirmation, and we accept the *'Athanasian'* Creed as the orthodox statement of Trinitarian doctrine and Christology.

6 - The Holy Scriptures

1 - The Holy Scriptures, that is, the writings of the Old and New Testaments, are writings inspired by the Spirit of God; these are accepted as canonical, and they form the basis of doctrinal formulations.

315

PREMISES OF THE FAITH

2 - The collection of writings together known as the Apocrypha is likewise regarded as canonical. This collection is employed for the quality of its teaching and example, but no doctrine is founded upon it.

7 - The Church

1 - Physically, the Church is the People of God: it is the community of the New Covenant. Spiritually, the Church is the Mystical Body of Christ: Christ is its head, and we, the baptised, are its members.

2 - The Church is called a Holy Nation, a Royal Priesthood, the Pillar and Ground of Truth. In the Nicene Creed, the Church is described as One, Holy, Catholic, and Apostolic.

3 - The Church is One, because all its members believe equally in One Lord, One Faith, One Baptism, One God and Father of us all. It is one Body, under one Head, Jesus Christ.

4 - The Church is Holy, because the Holy Spirit fills it, directs it, and consecrates its members.

5 - The Church is Catholic, because the Faith taught by Jesus Christ and the Church founded by him are for all people, for all time, everywhere.

6 - The Church is Apostolic, because it teaches and safeguards the Faith which Christ entrusted to his Apostles, and because it continues in the fellowship and mission of the Apostles.

COME AND WORSHIP

8 - The Communion of Saints

1 - The Communion of Saints is the spiritual union which exists between every Christian and Christ, and thus between every Christian. It is the fellowship of believers, past, present and future.

2 – Members of the Communion of Saints are in contact with one another through the medium of prayer.

9 - The Ministry of the Laity

1 - It is the office and dignity of Lay Persons – that is, of members of the Church who are not ordained – to represent Christ and his Church to the world, at all times and in all places, according to the measure of the especial and particular gifts with which they have been endowed, and to share in the life, work and worship of the Church.

10 – The Ministry of those in Holy Orders

1 - It is the office and dignity of those in Minor Ministries to represent Christ and his Church according to the measure of their gifts, with due witness and seemly example, and with proper regard for the reputation and right conduct of their ministry.

2 - It is the office and dignity of a Deacon to represent Christ and his Church, particularly as a servant of those in need; to minister at the altar; to proclaim the Gospel; to preach; and in the

PREMISES OF THE FAITH

absence of the Priest to baptise.

3 - It is the office and dignity of a priest to represent Christ and his Church, particularly as shepherd to the people; to celebrate the Eucharist; to bless; to preside; to anoint; to absolve; to preach; and to baptize.

4 - It is the office and dignity of a Bishop to represent Christ and his Church, particularly as chief priest and shepherd of a diocese; to consecrate; to ordain others to continue Christ's ministry; to celebrate the Eucharist; to anoint; to bless; to loose and to bind; to baptize and to confirm; to preside; to interpret and to judge; to guard the faith and unity of the whole Church; to proclaim God's word; to act in Christ's name for the peace of the world and for the strengthening and positive growth of the Community of the New Covenant.

11 - Prayer

1 - Prayer is conversation with God: a response to God by thought, with or without words.

2 - Christian prayer is a response to God the Father, through Jesus Christ, in the power of the Holy Spirit.

3 - The principal forms of prayer may be classified as Adoration, Praise, Thanksgiving, Penitence, Oblation, Intercession, and Petition.

4 - In Adoration our hearts are lifted to God,

COME AND WORSHIP

seeking nothing but the light of God's presence.

5 - In Praise we acknowledge and acclaim God's great glory, his holiness, his wonderful acts, his greatness, his power.

6 - In Thanksgiving we acknowledge every blessing of this life, every good and true thing that shapes our path, everything that brings us closer to God.

7 - In Penitence we make confession of our failings, with the intention of amendment.

8 - In Oblation we offer ourselves, all that we are, and all that we do, to God.

9 - In Intercession we pray for the needs of others.

10 - In Petition we pray for our own needs.

Awareness of God's presence shapes the response of prayer. In adoration we praise God for what he does and who he is. 'Hallowed be your name' asks that God be God, a petition that seeks blessing not for us, but for him. God's holiness demands confession of sin; his grace invites supplication for pardon. We seek his will, not our own, as we bring our petitions for guidance, provision, deliverance, and vindication. The communion of prayer deepens faith and love for God, not only as we draw near to him, but as we reach out in intercession for our fellow Christians and for a lost world.

New Dictionary of Theology,
Prayer, Theology of.

PREMISES OF THE FAITH

12 -- The Sacraments

1 - A sacrament is a visible form of invisible grace; that is to say, a sacrament is an outward and visible sign of an inward and spiritual grace.

2 - The Sacraments are seven in number:

Baptism,
Confirmation,
Eucharist,
Matrimony,
Penance,
Anointing,
Ordination.

3 - Of these, Baptism and Eucharist are Gospel Sacraments, instituted by Christ himself.

4 - Baptism is birth into the New Life, the Life of Grace, and incorporates us into Christ. It makes us members of Christ's Church, and heirs to God's Kingdom. A person is baptised with water, in the Name of the Father and of the Son and of the Holy Spirit.

5 - Confirmation strengthens us in the Life of Grace entered upon in Baptism. In confirmation we dedicate ourselves to Christ by conscious and willing choice; and in confirmation we receive, within our souls, the power of the Holy Spirit, who brings the seven-fold gift of wisdom, of understanding, of counsel, of might, of knowledge, of godliness, and of reverence.

6 - Through his redemptive sacrifice Christ gained

COME AND WORSHIP

for us the forgiveness of sins and the gift of life in abundance. That is why the Eucharist, which makes the sacrifice of Christ ever present to the People of God, is the central sacrament of the Church. The Holy Eucharist is the continual remembrance of Christ's life, death, and resurrection, until his coming again. In the Eucharist we are united with Christ in mystic communion, we are renewed in the life of grace, and our unity with all Christ's Church is deepened and strengthened.

7 - Because Matrimony is the counterpart of the oneness of Christ with his Church, marriage presents that union to us in visible form. It is, in essence, a rite of blessing that dignifies human love and makes it holy. In the ceremony, the couple are the ministers, the priest the witness.

8 - The Sacrament of Penance removes the sin which damages our life and our spiritual nature, and restores us to a state of harmony with God.

9 - Anointing or Holy Unction ensures Christ's help in circumstances of sickness. The Sacrament is not only given in preparation for transition, when it is called Extreme Unction, but is also used more generally by us to aid in the restoration of health.

10 - Ordination is the rite in which authority and the power of the Holy Spirit are given to those being received into Holy Orders.

321

PREMISES OF THE FAITH

13 - Adoption in the Beloved

1 - It is the certain faith of the Catholic Church that the sovereign purpose of Christ's Incarnation, his life, death, passion, resurrection and ascension, is that we might come to share his divinity. For Christ humbled himself to share our humanity, that we might become children of God by adoption through him; that the image of God within us, marred by failings, might be restored to its shining, unsullied and original splendour; that we might have true part in the life of God, not, indeed, through union with God's essence, but through our total participation in the outpouring of God's grace.

Praise be to the God and Father of our Lord Jesus Christ, who has blessed us in the heavenly realms with every spiritual blessing in Christ. For he chose us in him before the world began, to be holy and without blame in his sight. In love he predestined us to be adopted as his sons through Jesus Christ, in accordance with his pleasure and will; to the praise of his glorious grace which he has freely given us in the Beloved.

Ephesians, 1:3-6

Jesus is "the new man" (see Eph 4:24; Col 3:10) who calls redeemed humanity to share in His divine life. The mystery of the Incarnation lays the foundations for an anthropology which, reaching beyond its own limitations and contradictions, moves towards God Himself, indeed towards the goal of divinization. This occurs through the grafting of the redeemed on to Christ and their admission into the intimacy of the Trinitarian life. The Fathers have laid great stress on this soteriological dimension of the mystery of the Incarnation: it is only because the Son of God truly

COME AND WORSHIP

became man that man, in him and through him, can truly become a son of God.

Pope John Paul II,
Novo Millennio Ineunte, 23

14 - The Great Assurance

1 - As Christians we are privileged to live in Newness of Life, of Abundance of Life, working for the Kingdom, praying, and watching for the coming of our Lord.

2 - And we have this assurance: that nothing, not even death, is able to separate us from the Love of God which is in Christ Jesus.

'The Spirit and the Bride say, Come! And let the one who hears say, Come! Whoever is thirsty, let that one come; and whoever wishes, let that one take freely of the waters of life'.

Revelation, 22:17